MEDIOCRE LEADERSHIP

HINDERING ENGAGEMENT, GROWTH, AND PRODUCTIVITY

Dr. JAMES MCLAUGHLIN, DBA

Published by: Dr. James McLaughlin Jr., DBA | DuPont, Georgia, USA

For information about buying this title in bulk quantities, or for special sales opportunities (which may include electronic versions; custom cover designs; and content particular to your business, training goals, marketing focus, or branding interests), please contact us at www.1teamintl.com, info@1teamintl.com, or 855-461-8326.

Library of Congress Control Number (LCCN #): 2021912905

ISBN: 978-1-63760-957-6(Paperback) | ISBN: 978-1-63760-964-4 (ePUB)

Limit of Liability/Disclaimer of Warranty: The publisher and the author make no representations or warranties with respect to the accuracy or completeness of the contents of this work and specifically disclaim all warranties, including without limitation warranties of fitness for a particular purpose. No warranty may be created or extended by sales or promotional materials. The advice and strategies contained herein may not be suitable for every situation. This work is sold with the understanding that the publisher is not engaged in rendering legal, accounting, or other professional services. If professional assistance is required, the services of a competent professional person should be sought. Neither the publisher nor the author shall be liable for damages arising here from. The fact that an organization or website is referred to in this work as a citation and/or a potential source of further information does not mean that the author or the publisher endorses the information the organization or website may provide or recommendations it may make. Further, readers should be aware that internet websites listed in this work may have changed or disappeared between when this work was written and when it is read.

Printed in the United States of America

This book is printed on acid-free paper.

ABOUT THE AUTHOR

Entrepreneur, Management Consultant, Author, Scholar, and Educator are just a few titles associated with Dr. James McLaughlin and his business initiatives. His foundation originates in the Signal Corp of the United States Army, along with numerous years of Department of Defense Information Technology contract work. With extensive support of the U.S. military in the Middle East and Kyrgyzstan, Dr. McLaughlin provides a wealth of real-world business knowledge and global experience to organizational development, growth, and sustainability.

Additionally, serving as an influencer and consultant for small business development for the disadvantaged or deprived communities throughout the nation, an explicit aspiration for a level playing field and equality is a vital point of interest for Dr. McLaughlin. "Business creativity is essential, and with the right structure and analysis, the less fortunate can strive in the business market and create economic stability for their families and ultimately the communities in which they reside." This quote by Dr. McLaughlin is one of many that exemplifies his desire to help entrepreneurs grow. Thus, Dr. McLaughlin's writing style adds a vital tool for business leaders and the potentials to capitalize on opportunities with minimal investments.

Also, with his teaching and administration experiences throughout China, Dr. McLaughlin adds educational consulting to his list of competencies and services. In education, he develops customized business curriculums and process improvement strategies to support Secondary schools, International schools, Private schools, and Universities as well as provides support to individual students for the various business exams. As a collaborative instructional leader, Dr. McLaughlin assists teachers and administrators with instructional strategies and coaching for optimal student achievement.

Dr. McLaughlin holds a DBA in Global Business and Leadership and an MBA from California Intercontinental University, a Master of Arts in Industrial-Organizational Psychology from Touro University Worldwide, a Master of Science in Innovation and Entrepreneurship, and a Bachelor of Science in Entertainment Business from Full Sail University. He also completed his Principal Certificate training at the prestigious Lamar University located in Beaumont, Texas. It is through extensive education and real-world practical application that inspires him to write on business topics that can help entrepreneurs and small business leaders move forward efficiently.

With Mediocre Leadership, his sole objective is to present awareness of the impact a good leader can have on a person, a TEAM, or an entire project. By understanding how a mediocre leader functions, organizational leaders and people of influence can make value-based decisions that directly contribute to the vision, mission, and success of a firm. Thus, streamlining efficiency through effective organizational structure, communications, and inspiration.

TABLE OF CONTENTS

LIST OF TABLES

LIST OF FIGURES

FOREWORD

Mediocre leadership couldn't have been published at a better time. A world in upheavals calls for strong leadership unlike any time since World War Two. Leaders and would-be leaders are in need of a reminder of what true leadership is and, just as importantly what it is not. This book cuts to the quick and provides the reader with a no-nonsense approach of how to best navigate the leadership issues that need to be addressed in a complex world—a world characterized by globalization and specialization where technological advancement and human ingenuity are developing at unparalleled rates.

This book illustrates how much changes need to be harnessed, tamed, and directed by effective leadership if organizations want to continue to thrive as they are propelled into the uncertainty of the mid-twenty-first century.

Dr. James McLaughlin brings his experience and expertise to exemplify what organizations must do to avoid mediocrity and ineffectiveness in leadership. He draws upon his sound doctoral-level academic background, his experience in the military, his work in the world of business, and his role as a master educator to bear on what is his best book yet. Identifiable and relatable anecdotes from multi-national organizations are used to prove that even Goliaths can be struck down if they settle for mediocrity. More importantly, Mediocre leadership provides tangible commonsense solutions to ensure organizations have leaders who can avoid such pitfalls.

One of the great joys experienced in reading this book is the straightforward language that is accessible for leaders who are not versed in leadership academia or have vast experiences within an organization. In a time when authors tend to beat around the bush, this book offers a no-holds-barred approach that is engaging and refreshing as it addressed the economic, cultural, and ethical realities leaders today must come to terms with.

I have been an educational leader for over twenty years. I found myself nodding along as I read this book. It is evident that it is designed for all leaders, not just those who live in the for-profit world. One of my great pleasures in my role is sharing my knowledge and experience with people who are fledging leaders. I will be gifting them this book and putting it on their must-read list.

Michael Brown

Educator and Author

PREFACE

Leadership is an attribute of a person that can make or break the outcome of a business model or endeavor. With outstanding leadership, companies flourish locally and extend their services internationally with an enhanced vision, mission, and broadened purpose. Such leadership encompasses the moral character, respect, discipline, and dignity required to lead people in any industry. There is an expectancy of value-based decision-making, sufficient planning, process maturity, and project discipline when effective leadership is in place. Thus, highlighting the efficient and practical measures that strong leaders must take to become, remain, and help influence others with achieving success.

As a professional that has led in various industries that include the United States Army, numerous Department of Defense (DoD) contractor firms, commercial organizations, private companies, education, and management consulting, the one constant similarity pertained to leadership. While some of these entities or organizations maintained well-mature leadership structures, others seemed to miss this opportunity, which was evident with continuous turmoil and inefficiencies, highlighting how essential good leaders are for organizational growth and personnel success.

Mediocre Leadership takes a look into how mediocre leaders think, function, and perform in various industries. It engages not only what mediocre leaders do but how they think during normal, tactical, and strategic operations. With an educated understanding of such, aspiring entrepreneurs, business owners, and company leaders can modify their approach using real-world instances and models. Additionally, this book streamlines a process to becoming a value-based leader by clearly pinpointing a mediocre leader's characteristics. Consequently, it provides a framework of best practices to help business owners and leaders reach their full potential most efficiently.

Nevertheless, with experiences working in foreign locations that include Kuwait, Kyrgyzstan, and China, to name a few, my leadership experiences serve as strategic assets for organizational, operational, and personal success. Additionally, with various degrees that include a Master of Science in Innovation and Entrepreneurship, a general MBA, a Master of Arts in Industrial/Organizational Psychology, a Master of Education in Administration, and a DBA in Global Business and Leadership, I offer a well-rounded practical and theoretical approach to the topics of entrepreneurship, leadership, TEAMwork, and functioning in the global market. Regardless, Mediocre Leadership welcomes current and new entrepreneurs to our fraternity of leaders that set the standard for organizational development, growth, and sustainability.

Dr. James McLaughlin, DBA

Author | Management Consultant | Entrepreneur

US+ 1 (855) 46–1TEAM ext. 2

www.1teamintl.com

INTRODUCTION

There is a growing perplexity about the expanding space of mediocre leadership in the current corporate environment. There are many technically savvy executives and proficient specialists who are highly driven but are, in reality, "part-time" leaders because they know so little about leadership and actually do not like what they consider as the "drudgery of leadership work." Generally, for external observers, the quandary is perhaps amplified by the misconception that the growing level of global sophistication and innovation, which is a reflection of increasing human ingenuity, should by extension also be a reflection of the advancing state of leadership excellence in corporate organizations—especially since most innovative products and services are seen to be promoted by organized corporate bodies. However, individual ingenuity and technical expertise do not always translate into strong leadership capabilities. There are perhaps more innovative products and services on the market whose potentials have been truncated by mediocre leadership and ineffective TEAMs than there are successful products and services.

To buttress the point, a recent study published in 2018 reveals that 55% of the organizations surveyed believe their leaders are mediocre; ironically, about 80% of the organizations surveyed didn't know what to do. Most organizations today are confused about how to tackle mediocre leadership and its adverse effect on their corporate cultures. Sophisticated investors know that apart from the track record and hard data on earnings, when they invest their money in a venture, they are actually banking on the quality of the TEAM and the competence of the leadership that will get the job done. Many companies operating in competitive environments have had to pay fatal prices due to late discoveries and belated changes to problematic leadership gaps, while many start-ups simply didn't have a fighting chance to survive market entry or scale their business. In other organizations, frequent leadership changes have become commonplace, especially when the existence and future of the company are threatened. However, with the increasing number of scandals, corrupt practices, sexual harassment, and many other forms of unethical behaviors, there is a need to hold leaders to higher standards and also apply much higher standards to ourselves.

What then are the known attributes of mediocre leaders? How can we avoid mediocre leadership? And how do we tackle a mediocre culture? These are some of the fundamental questions that the information in this book will robustly address. It is impractical to address a problem that is not properly understood and contextualized; this is why an extensive introspection into the anatomy of mediocre leadership, its underlying characteristics, overt inclinations, and adverse effects is crucial and has been undertaken in this book. Change is a complex process that requires tact and an abundance of caution because of the delicate implications it could have if not properly managed. Tackling mediocre leadership and culture in an organization could involve lay-offs and radical changes; still, it is important to bear in mind that high employee turnover could cause serious product and service disruptions that can result in customer defection for businesses in highly competitive industries. More so, changes that trigger employee panic and low job satisfaction could deflate organizational morale. This could, in turn, create a downward spiral of poor product and service delivery, decline in earnings, and the growth of rumors and horror stories that could unsettle investors and further lead to a fall in the company's stock value.

This is why organizations should be careful about implementing radical changes in one fell swoop. They should instead start at the top and work their way to the lower layers of the organization. Fundamentally, experts agree that mediocrity is essentially a symptom of ineffective leadership and not primarily a problem of the organization's personnel. A mediocre leader will create a mediocre culture, which will, in turn, create more mediocre leaders and employees, and this is how the vicious cycle continues. In order to break the cycle of mediocrity, corporate bodies must begin with a change of leadership where necessary. They must also avoid appointing people with mediocre leadership qualities into vacant positions and must have a good grasp of what qualities to look out for and those to avoid. It is important that the attributes of mediocrity that leaders could exhibit are properly understood so that broader organizational initiatives, strategies, and actions can be taken to correct or eliminate such attributes from the rank and file. Organizations looking to understand the nature, manifestations, and workings of mediocre leadership will find this book a resourceful tool.

Readers will learn about the Peter Principle, which elucidates on the common practice of leaders being continually promoted until they reach their level of incompetence. This emphasizes the need for continuous exposure and learning, even for the best leaders. Explored in chapter one are topics on the portrait of a mediocre leader, why we have mediocre leaders and cultures, and hints about the politics that perpetuate mediocre leadership. Addressed in chapter two are topics on recognizing mediocre thinking, knowing the stages of competence development, and understanding the roles of theoretical and practical knowledge in leadership. In chapter three, topics like the Grape Vine Effect, the indispensable communication functions that mediocre leaders lack, and other vital discourses on communication, such as the communication process loop, are examined. Chapters four, five, and six address weighty factors that construe moral and ethical boundaries vis-à-vis the bankruptcy of mediocre leaders; emphasize the roles of rigidity, resistance to change, success-induced complacency, and other personal and organizational barriers in relation to mediocre leadership; and portray how the lack of adequate cognitive and metacognitive abilities, defects in the decision-making process, and micromanagement, contribute to inconsistent managerial practices and second-rate leadership.

Chapter seven delves into the narrow outlook, dogmatic mold, insular nature, and cultural disconnect associated with mediocre leadership. Chapter eight examines the traits of Self-Centered

Leadership (SCL) and how this could be related to the individualistic tendencies in our societal structure, particularly in Western cultures. Insights were also drawn from research on organizations in other cultures, such as from the Middle East. Chapter Nine unmasked the nature of remorseless and unsympathetic leadership and the value of empathy to leadership excellence. Chapter ten dwelt extensively on the relationship between mediocre leadership and mediocre culture, the vital qualities of excellent leaders, and how to cultivate a culture of excellence in an organization. There are also a number of other cogent issues and valuable information that leaders and stakeholders in organizations will find handy in this book in relation to their drive to enhance leadership delivery and stamp out mediocre leadership.

CHAPTER ONE

WHAT IS A MEDIOCRE LEADER, AND WHY DO MEDIOCRE LEADERS EXIST?

"No one gets ahead by striving for mediocrity."
— Glenn C. Stewart

Case Study: BlackBerry

Before Apple's iPhone arrived, the ultimate smartphone that everyone could get was a BlackBerry. In 1998, BlackBerry, with its line of smartphones and tablets, was a smashing success. It was in a class of its own – there seemed to be a sense of prestige around anyone with a BlackBerry. In fact, Google's first Android prototypes were described as BlackBerry clones. Back then, BlackBerry was appreciated for its superb security, reliable email, and utilitarian functionality. BlackBerry Messenger was also exceptional in its making, connecting more people in a way that had never been done before. The BlackBerry keyboard became an iconic part of mobile telephony history because of its effectiveness and popularity. Basically, BlackBerry dominated in the United States and had 20% of the global market. So, what happened to this giant mobile company? Why did it crumble?

The fall of BlackBerry can be traced back to early 2012. Although the company tried to manage its crash landing for a while, it almost seemed inevitable. While the whole mobile industry began to opt for much bigger touchscreen displays with the arrival of iPhone and Android, BlackBerry focused more on sticking with their usual size. Apple, and others like HTC and Samsung, jumped on the new track destination for mobile technology – i.e., bigger touchscreen displays; but BlackBerry chose to stay conservative and complacent. In essence, while the mobile industry was undergoing an evolution, BlackBerry's leadership could not see the bigger picture. Today, while these mobile companies continue to exploit the evolution to the fullest, BlackBerry is nowhere to be found. It has vanished into oblivion.

There are two main issues wrong with BlackBerry's leadership back then; they are—conservatism and complacency. Being conservative and seeking to appease existing customers were only half of the problem. In addition, BlackBerry exhibited hubris with disturbing regularity. In one such instance, it launched the PlayBook tablet without an email client on board. It insisted, alongside Adobe, that Flash would be the future of rich mobile content. It ended up delaying a spec-competitive smartphone release until it had a chip robust enough to handle Flash's requirements. BlackBerry seemed to believe that people would wait for its superior products or put up with the defects because it was BlackBerry. This haughtiness contributed to their fall. It is the very definition of mediocre thinking to assume that there is more room for error than possible.

That was BlackBerry, a company knowing that it had a lot of assets and advantages, and as a result, exhibited a reluctance to adapt to changes, flaunting consistent smugness about its past accomplishments. Blackberry also had a history of nepotism, which usually leads to mediocre, and in fact, poor leadership. The company was known to promote people from within based on tenure rather than on valuable skills and the potential to lead. This was another attribute of mediocre leadership and culture that characterized the organization.

It is important to note that once upon a time, Blackberry was the ultimate status symbol, and many people couldn't fathom using other phone brands; but today, BlackBerry has been edged out of a Smartphone market that it once helped to shape and define. It is a cautionary tale to companies: no matter how good you may already be, there is always the potential to do better, and if you are not willing to change and innovate, someone else will. Mediocre thinking won't keep you on the stage for long.

A Contextual Background

Sadly, mediocre leadership is more commonplace than a lot of people realize or are willing to admit. This is largely because they are carried away by the fascination of the technological boom, the mega successes of the big brands, and the fast-paced nature of our 21st-century economy that continuously flashes innovation, competition, and opportunities as the lifeblood of today's economies. However, the high rate of failing companies, businesses (and other forms of establishments), including the declining/ blanket rate of performance culture in many organizations, are clear pointers to the pervasive presence of mediocre leadership all around us. Though we should be grateful for the plethora of innovative tools and technologies that we have at our disposal today, we would have been worse off without them; however, we must realize that despite these tools, organizational or business failure is inevitable in the long run if people do not have the right thinking.

One of the startling ironies in today's business and corporate leadership environments, whether in the public or private sector, is that many people holding leadership positions do not actually like to do the "people work" or have no idea what it is about—but they sure like "to lead!" They like the sense of importance that comes from their work or undertakings, the perks of the office, and the opportunity to flex their ideas, technical expertise, ambition, or personal drive; but they lack the focal pivot of leadership, which is the ability to source, effectively manage, and efficiently propel human and material resources towards the achievement of set goals, objectives, and ideas. The absence of this is why we see a lot of burned-out people, talents, organizations, and businesses. Excellent leaders aren't people who are only buried in their technical expertise or big ambitions, but they are leaders who are clear about the big picture, regularly clarify complex issues, are efficient, and skillfully coordinate the best inputs and cooperation of TEAM members towards the achievement of visionary goals and objectives.

Excellent leadership requires individual capacity and competence, charisma and people skills, organizational skills, efficient management of resources, adaptive abilities to changing market environments, and the application of innovative thinking, tools, and techniques. M.R. Ahmed, in his analysis of the Emerging Leadership Theory (ELT), notes that leadership is both an art and a science. As an art it involves four pillars (4 Cs) of leadership: i.e., character, culture, communication, and charisma; and as a science, it requires an objective application of knowledge in leadership and decision-making processes, based on observation, experimentation, or available data. This requires that leaders can learn, unlearn, and relearn. This is why leadership shouldn't be thrust on people based on assumptions or their ability to deliver in certain specific areas, but it should be done based on an evaluation of the relevant skills that leaders need to deliver in the new roles they are undertaking. This explains why regular training programs are critical to organizational growth.

As Liebman (2016) has rightly observed, "When leadership is assigned or assumed—rather than earned and developed the optical focus turns to what and how—with no perception or awareness of why or purpose [sic]." Leadership in today's competitive environment, therefore, requires the most effective stimulation of people's responses and the efficient coordination of human and material resources towards the achievement of the organization's goals and objectives. Therefore, the pivotal challenge of leadership is having the right combination of skills required to propel the best of human responses and to see to the efficient deployment of resources towards the achievement of defined goals or objectives. The absence of such skills inevitably results in mediocre level performances in leadership, organizational outcomes, and culture.

The Portrait of a Mediocre Leader

Berman and West (2003) note that there is a need for more studies to distill the contextual nature and other relevant analyses of how mediocrity can be tackled, just like the concept of excellence has through scholarship gained clarity in its definition, with some consensus of the processes that can be employed to instill excellence in corporate leadership and management. There are some general ideas of what mediocrity in management looks like, such as leaders passing the buck, dodging responsibility, and artfully hiding behind rules, policies, and supposed misunderstandings in order to avoid being blamed. These leaders exercise persistent misjudgment of situations and thus make wrong decisions. They miss the core elements of the big picture due to misplaced legalism and thus get the organization entangled in problems that keep it from seizing valuable opportunities. They are also seen as people-pleasing compromisers who know and perform well enough to keep their jobs and even get promoted occasionally, but they do not record outstanding accomplishments because they do not go the extra mile to take the initiative. They are known to discourage employees who are different and more enterprising (Ashworth, 2001).

From surveys and responses involving over 1,800 respondents, leadership expert Vince Molinaro (2019) identifies five general characteristics that mediocre leaders consistently exhibit. These characteristics are discussed below, together with other well-known traits that pundits and analysts agree are trademarks of mediocre leaders.

1. **Willingness to blame others:** Mediocre leaders always pass the buck and are never willing to take responsibility when something goes wrong. They can be vicious in the blame game or simply point fingers at others, but they clearly do not take responsibility.

2. **They are selfish:** Selfishness is a character that is closely associated with leaders who care more about themselves than they do about others or the organization. Due to their self-centered attitude, it is not difficult to see why they do not go the extra mile, except to keep their jobs, get a promotion, or some other benefit. Self-centered leadership is less likely to proactively engage ideas, problems, or innovative thinking in order to advance the welfare of the organization and its people.

3. **Uncivil and mean:** Mediocre leaders are not culturally refined and believe that one way to secure their position in an organization is to exercise their strength and dominance. They are thus routinely disrespectful, lack empathy, and often insult and mistreat subordinates that work with them. Hot-headed, angry, and emotionally unstable bosses ruin things and push away valuable talent from an organization.

4. **They display ineptitude and compromise standards:** As we noted earlier, competence and capacity are indispensable factors in excellent leadership, and leaders who rise to positions that are above their skills, experience, and capabilities are less likely to provide inspiring leadership. This leads to poor performance and rubs off on the organization. Maintaining standards of excellence is an important virtue that successful leaders do not compromise. When leaders begin to compromise on excellence, their values, and their objectives, they have given in to mediocrity.

5. **They exhibit a lack of initiative:** Proactivity is an essential ingredient in the decision-making make-up of an organization and its leadership. Mediocre leaders delay, defer, procrastinate, and prevaricate on the job. They do not do much, but show up every day, avoid the hard decisions, and hope that nobody notices.

6. **They are not transparent:** Opaqueness is one of the attributes that mediocre leaders also exhibit. They are always changing the rules of the game, are partial, downplay the importance of merit, and give preferential treatment to their favorites. They have divisive tendencies and are somewhat sentimental in their decision-making.

7. **Inability to cultivate talent and human resource:** Mediocre leaders are blind to the potentials, uniqueness, and abilities of their staff, but excellent leaders do everything to know the strengths, weaknesses, and potentials of their staff in order to develop and deploy them for the most suitable roles that will help them become their best. Under mediocre leaders, the opportunities to discover new roles and career paths are stifled.

8. **They are close-minded and do not evaluate feedback:** Mediocre leaders are not open to ideas from others, they are very insensitive, they insist on hierarchical relations, and they aren't responsive to their TEAM. This coerces subordinates into a culture of silence and kills initiative. Feedback from within and outside the organization is critical to the survival of any organization. When leaders close their ears to feedback from employees, customers, and industry experts, they cannot adapt to changing realities and are likely to run their organizations aground.

9. **They do not delegate authority:** Mediocre leaders are afraid to delegate authority but are more comfortable with delegating tasks when they are overwhelmed. They always want to be in control and do not want anybody to share their position with them. This slows down their productivity and weakens their effectiveness. Excellent leaders know the importance of delegating authority in order to enhance the productivity of their TEAM.

10. **Inability to communicate vision/objectives and translate knowledge into tangibles:** Mediocre leaders fundamentally do not have a good grip on the vision. Their understanding is more mechanical than real, and as a result, they are not able to translate the knowledge they have into tangible deliverables and results. They are more prone to following established patterns and find it difficult to tackle and clarify complex issues. They cannot clearly communicate the vision, which hampers the ability to translate unclear objectives into action plans. Communication is an essential tool in leadership, and leaders who are defective in their communication abilities are inevitably capped at a mediocre level. To break the ice, they need to develop sound communication skills and practicality in their approach to problem-solving.

Organizational Mediocrity

The impact of mediocre leadership on an organization is that it infects the organization with the same mediocre mindsets and attitudes, and this leads to a mediocre culture. Below are major signs that your organization has fallen into a mediocre culture and that its leadership needs to be reorganized to expand the thinking space and the attitude of your people. It is important to note that a change in leadership does not automatically translate to an excellent organizational culture, but it is the first step towards bringing about the desired change.

1. **Your managers are more absorbed in technical work than in leading the people:** Technical expertise is an important ingredient in leadership and should not be jettisoned at any rate; but leaders aren't supposed to be buried in the minutest details and activities in the technical departments or field, hereby losing valuable time. Instead, they should be thinking up strategic plans, preparing for the future, clarifying vital questions, and

communicating the vision and objectives to employees. Leaders are supposed to create room for their subordinates to develop, grow their skills, and attend to the fine technical details. They are to coach their TEAMs through the various phases of the organization's growth and oversee the overall fulfillment of the aims and objectives of the organization and its projects. The reality that analysts have pointed out is that most leaders do not enjoy the leadership work and would rather get involved in their areas of technical expertise in order not to feel out of place.

However, strong leaders know the value of sitting at the head of the table and helping to coordinate the TEAM towards achieving its goals. The technical expertise that they bring to the table is valuable, but their leadership capability in leading the TEAM to success is the truest measure of their value to the TEAM. Leaders must be on top of the most significant priorities, delegate authority to subordinates in other areas of importance, create clarity for their TEAM by consistently communicating core and specific priorities and evaluating progress made on the job.

2. **Conservative leadership culture:** If you have managers who are more conservative and traditional in their approach to leadership than they are to achieving results, your organization then operates within a mediocre culture. Such environments do not sufficiently engage employees to sample their opinions and get their inputs, especially because of command-and-control walls created by the managers. Managers who see employees as people who are only to take orders are rewarded by their paychecks and who should not speak much except to give reports on their assigned tasks are mediocre leaders. This also is reflected through micro-managing, poor responses to feedback, or total disregard for it. They also exhibit a lack

of empathy, show no appreciation when necessary, and are poor coaches for their subordinates. Successful leaders know the value of employee engagement, and because they know leadership is about people, they spend their time giving direction, boosting the morale of their staff, and providing vital support systems. They also encourage inputs from employees and ensure to show appreciation to their staff for their good work. Generally, by connecting with their employees and also establishing vital relations with key members of staff that have strategic relevance or man sensitive positions, leaders are better able to stimulate the best responses from those who work for them and can adapt their management style to suit their unique corporate make-up.

3. **Your managers are preoccupied with tolerating low performers than focusing on the best employees:** Cultivating and coaching TEAM members to peak performance is an essential part of leadership. However, when managers spend an undue amount of time disciplining or tolerating low performers, mediocrity becomes prevalent. When employees do not meet expected standards, leaders should engage them in a process that coaches them and not tolerate such inferior standards. However, they also do not go on retaining underperforming employees who are not developing because they know it is bound to have an adverse effect on the work culture and performance of the TEAM.

Great cultures do not tolerate mediocre performance. They make the necessary investments but also take the tough decisions necessary to sustain high performance. In situations of underperformance, mediocre leaders are more evasive, tend to avoid crucial discussions with defaulting employees and do not employ a coaching attitude when approaching employees that need to learn. This is because of their limited people skills and their command-and-control consciousness.

4. **You are losing high performers:** High performers can recognize a mediocre culture when they see one. Their initial response may be to take on the challenge of putting up ideas and initiatives to management in order to change the status quo, but where that proves negative, and they find themselves being increasingly sucked into the mediocre culture, they will leave! Those who stay because they have nowhere else to go in the immediate will leave at the slightest opportunity they have.

   Mediocre managers create mediocre and complacent TEAMs that keep innovation, competence, hard work, and exceptional results out of the organization. This becomes an albatross and frustrates talented members of the TEAM who either adjust to the mediocre culture or become restless and take their leave. Average results don't inspire talented employees, as they need to always exercise themselves on tasks that challenge their creativity and innovative abilities. This is what exceptional leaders effectively utilize as they set clear standards and deadlines that they expect their employees to meet. They challenge their TEAM positively, reward high performers, and show in their actions that average performance is not acceptable.

5. **When leaders avoid confronting challenging situations:** A mediocre culture is one in which there is a hush about confronting challenging situations because of their delicate or complex nature. Leaders, managers, and employees alike are more comfortable with staying in their comfort zones and taking the path of least resistance. Candidness, honesty, and pragmatism are supplanted by a culture of sycophancy, silence, procrastination, and lack of action. A proactive culture deals with challenges head-on, takes action and deals with emerging issues early

before they become too big or insurmountable. This helps to keep the TEAM focused and sustain the big picture in their minds as they navigate different situations. Such high-performance responses must begin with the leaders and must be transmitted as a culture throughout the organization. This doesn't allow situations to fester that could undermine the energy, performance, and productivity of the organization.

6. **Politics of Inversion:** Hermanowicz (2013), in his analysis of the mediocre culture in organizations, explains an inverted situation in which mediocrity is maintained by a key social process that ensures the marginalization of the adept members of the workforce, while rewards are clandestinely subverted in favor of those with less capability. This actually results from a situation in which those of average abilities are in the majority and must decide on what to do with the few who are high performers. The tensions lead to a situation in which high performers are marginalized for their behavior, while the system is skewed to protect the threatened position of the mediocre TEAM members. Marginalization can come in the form of unfounded disparities in the allocation of resources to units, departments, or officers with respect to the discharge of their responsibilities. Other forms could be mockery, intimidation, and provocation. The list below captures elements of the marginalization culture and politics as documented by Hermanowicz (2013).

Table 1.1 Hermanowicz's List of Marginalization Elements

- Institutionalized politics in which the reward system has been altered to make it inconsistent with institutional goals and favors the loyalty of mediocre workers.

- Recognition by the adept of their minority status and absence of a "critical mass" necessary for institutional functioning.
- A pervasiveness of control in which much of, if not all, of the group's life, has been altered by a reconfiguration of the reward system.
- A social organization of the less able through which they coordinate and communicate their activities among one another.
- Recognition of the importance of articulating meritocratic norms so that those who raise questions and objections are marginalized, whereas those who are quiet are rewarded.
- The concern that the reconfiguration of the reward system, if at all, through drastic measures, would entail "cleaning house" and installing "ethical" leaders and high-performing subordinates.
- The idea that marginalization protects others whose status would be eroded by the achievements of the adept.
- The perception that those who protest are further marginalized.
- The practice of recruiting new members of the group who will, immediately or eventually, conform to the beliefs and values of the average, thereby maintaining their majority and control of power.

- A realization that one can neither be expelled easily nor can anyone voluntarily remove himself easily from the group. There is an element of permanency in membership.

Why We Have Mediocre Leaders

A high-performance culture must begin at the top of an organization and trickle down to the other layers of the organization, however as we have already observed, most leaders at the top of their organizations were not picked because of their leadership abilities or experience. This observation has become commonplace with analysts and experts who study organizational culture and leadership. These leaders could indeed be good at other things, but as they say, "he is not just great with people." That someone is good at what they do, whether in a law firm, hospital, sales shop, or in an area of knowledge, does not automatically transform them into good leaders. Though their knowledge makes them leading voices and opens a platform for them to provide leadership, but possessing the right combination of skills needed in the new position and for the responsibilities that come with it should be the priority in appointing people to positions of leadership. We must get to that point where we realize that people simply cannot give what they don't have. It is that simple.

This is the first problem that people who want to transform their organizations must think of. When we do not choose leaders based on their leadership abilities but allow a narrow focus on their areas of strength or certain sentimental notions to dictate our choices, we are more likely to settle for mediocre leadership. Areas of strength matter in so far as the leadership requirements would not demand more; however, it is good advice to choose leaders based on their abilities and the demands that would be made on them. What many organizations do is to choose a few folks and rush them into a training course in order to implant in them over a couple of days important life skills that they don't have an innate propensity for. Good leadership choices are better made when the prospective candidates have clear potentials and inclinations that can be further enhanced through developmental courses, instead of picking just anybody and hoping that the courses will change them. Observation reveals that many people do not want to be people leaders; they only take the job because of the prestige, but even after they have the job, they still do not want to be a leader of personnel. Though everyone can get better at learning how to improve their people and leadership skills, they must have an inner desire to want to do that.

Another reason we have mediocre leaders prevailing at the top of many organizations is that most of the organizations that have produced them in the first place are mediocre. They are a product of the system and therefore reflect the values, culture, and nature of the system. As we have seen in the analysis of Hermanowicz (2013), once new members with promising attributes come into a mediocre culture and begin to exhibit a culture of excellence, honesty, or bring up new ideas, the culture either becomes hostile or its lackluster attitude naturally snobs this new energy until it blends in with the prevalent mediocre culture. It takes bold and courageous CEOs, executives, and managers to alter the narrative and change the culture. Courageous leaders must show by words and actions that mediocrity is no longer acceptable, and they must take effective steps to promote a high-performance culture. As these new traits are encouraged, people will begin to respond based on the examples of the new leadership drive. Those who follow you will only follow what you do and not what you say; words must be backed by action.

If you do not reward exceptional performance but accept average performance, then the norm will become average. Incentivizing excellence and rejecting average is another important value-adding step that helps to reform a system and culture. Set higher standards and insist on people rising to meet those standards, and you will begin to see a change in the culture within the organization. Mediocre leaders remain only because we do not set high standards for them to meet. It might be important to create an opportunity for them to upgrade their skills; however, it is important to benchmark your performance at excellence if you want them to excel. Leadership is not easy and requires a lot of work. It will require consistency, a good focus on people, and regular assessment of organizational performance. Leaders must show courage to broach important conversations and check on the welfare of their subordinates for the sake of the culture. Exceptional leaders understand that their decisions or indecisions have a strong effect on their corporate culture.

The Cyclical Impact of Mediocrity on an Organization

As we progress in this book, more on the nature of organizational mediocrity will be expatiated, and suggestions would be made on how to avoid or correct its limiting effect. However, it is important to quickly note that organizational mediocrity has negative consequences that adversely impact not only the internal relationships but also the external relationships of the organization. From employees to customers, suppliers, and stakeholders, organizational mediocrity affects the relationships between these different players in the life of an organization. The following is a chart that shows how mediocrity can affect a for-profit company, its employees, suppliers, and customers.

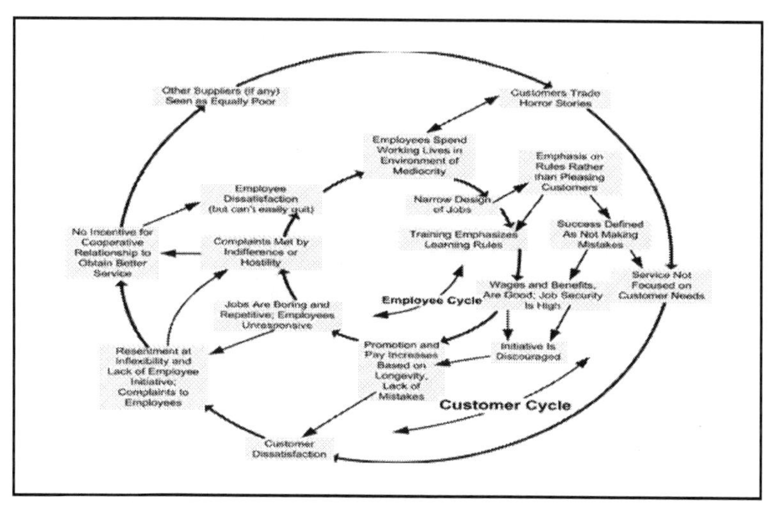

Fig 1.1 How Mediocrity can Affect a For-Profit Company, its Employees, Suppliers, and Customers (Source: Heidrich & Rethi, 2012)

CHAPTER TWO

INADEQUATE PRACTICAL OR THEORETICAL ABILITIES

"Real knowledge is to know the extent of one's ignorance"
—Confucius.

Case Study: Blockbuster

The video rental business was immensely profitable from the start. It had grown organically, without the support of startups and Venture Capitalists chasing the vague promise of potential wealth. Video gave its consumers the ability to time-shift programming, which was like getting released from a kind of entertainment prison. With this feeling, there was an opportunity for manufacturers to charge a lot for VCRs. The studios realized this and chose to price the tapes ludicrously high, which did not work so well.

Back then, the model was simple: higher rentals meant having the right titles in the right stores at the right times. This meant that retailers could make even more money via improvements in distribution and inventory management. Blockbuster soon entered the market as a video-rental company. When Blockbuster acquired those independent stores, it could pool its supply and transaction data, which yielded some operational efficiencies. After Viacom acquired it in 1994, the company recruited some senior Walmart executives to deliver more operational brilliance. It applied Big Data insights about customer needs before there was a term for it. In-store selections got better.

Blockbuster was at its peak in 2004. The company survived the change from VHS to DVD. So what went wrong? The truth is that they failed to innovate into a market; they failed to see the new trend. People did not like to go to the store to buy CDS anymore, but instead, they preferred to rent or buy online and receive it at their doorsteps. Blockbuster did not only lose its customers to Netflix, but it also failed to make the transition to the new world. They failed to open up to new areas of expertise.

While Netflix was shipping out DVDs to their consumer's homes, Blockbuster thought their physical stores were enough to please their customers. Since they had been leading the movie rental market for years, the leadership did not see why they should change their strategy.

In 2000, Netflix founder, Reed Hastings, was said to have sent a partnership proposal to the former CEO of Blockbuster, John Antioco. Netflix was interested in Blockbuster in order to advertise their brand in the stores, with a plan that Netflix would run Blockbuster online. However, this idea got rejected by Antioco because he thought it was simply ridiculous and that Netflix's business model was a "niche business." This perception, however, came from a huge deficit in the working knowledge of the suggested model. Unknown to him then, Hasting's idea would have saved Blockbuster. Imagine having the opportunity to transform your business and turning it down. What the leadership of Blockbuster exhibited was an inadequate understanding of the trends and the progression of innovation in their industry. In 2010, Blockbuster filed for bankruptcy, with Netflix growing from strength to strength.

So, what lessons can be learned from Blockbuster's fall? First, understand the business you do and its industry. Blockbuster considered itself to be in the entertainment distribution business, but it was all about retail customer experience. Second, always keep an eye on the big picture. It is essential to be open to new areas of expertise in your business and to learn how new developments and innovations work.

It is important to reiterate that excellent leadership requires a combination of different components and factors, part of which includes that the leader possesses the relevant skillset needed to make qualitative inputs and deliver optimum results on the job. Excellent leadership is only possible when there is the right combination of knowledge, abilities, and experience suited to the level of performance that the job requires or the peculiar demands of the organization.

The competitive nature of our contemporary environments is amplified by the amazing rate of technological growth and development. Though, despite the abundant level of knowledge access and the number of tools, instruments, and equipment available, there are still serious concerns stemming from observations on the mediocre and incompetence levels in organizations. It is important to note that in the evolving global economic order that is increasingly inclined towards the flow of intellectual capital, individuals and their organizations are influenced by the environment to keep up with the necessary innovative outlook that secures their survival and success in the market.

However, for many, this is a struggle since they seem contained in a culture that is more reactive in its cycle of engagement. They operate on an average frequency that inclines them to do only the needful to keep their doors open as a going concern. This makes proactivity and innovation less likely and limits the resourceful abilities of the people. Such organizations may be susceptible to the vagaries of the business environment and the constant flux that characterizes it, except and until the unstable environmental conditions meet an equal match in resourcefulness, credence, innovation, and prompt action from within the organization. From the beginning of this Century up till now, analysis and studies have never shied to point to the pervasive gaps in competence in a large swathe of the regular businesses and organizations that we interact with on a daily basis (Wenig, 2004; Grudin, 2016).

Astute leaders know that 21st-century dynamics create knowledge obsolescence gaps for those who haven't imbibed the concept of lifelong learning. Leaders and businessmen who were happy to have "completed" their education or permanently earned a certification that claims they have certain skills by now have realized how wrong they were. The fact is that we have come to terms with the realities experts and industry analysts since the turn of the century have been pointing out, which is that every industry and region of the world—whether in advanced economies or developing nations—is experiencing profound changes that have impacted on how human talent is managed (Amidon and Macnamara, 2000).

The need to constantly evaluate the knowledge and skills level of performing employees in relation to the knowledge and skills that they need at the new level they are being prospected for is vital for sustainability. It is also important that recruitment criteria are regularly updated to capture changing demands in the skills required for excellence. In many cases, those promoted to new positions of leadership have shown great performance in previous assignments but have not been thoroughly evaluated based on the demands of the new job title and the unfolding dynamics in their peculiar industries. This is especially relevant to the proliferation of Knowledge Intensive Sectors (KISs) in the emergent global value chains and within the general context of today's knowledge-driven economies (Mas-Machuca, 2014).

Beyond the deficiency in apposite knowledge and skills, mediocre leaders are also not able to see beyond the limitations of the information, and in myriad cases, to see through the technology-enamored strategies that they must grapple with. As a result of this, they do not show the necessary applicative abilities required to implement complex changes or lead novel initiatives. Their ability to act is limited by their inadequacy in the applicable understanding, capabilities, and tools that they need to be successful at directing and motivating others. This stalls their ability to lead their organizations to the right decisions. They also are unable to help members of their TEAM through the discipline of the knowledge management process for the development of their TEAM's human capital.

The Role of Theoretical and Practical Knowledge in Leadership

Both theoretical and practical knowledge need to be present in organizational leadership for it to operate above average limits. Content is important. Where mediocre leaders are deficient in the necessary theoretical and practical knowledge needed, their value as assets to the organization is diminished by their limited intelligence. At crucial junctures when they are supposed to bring their insights and enlightenment to bear, the lack of it could constitute a costly liability of ignorance. It could be in relation to a proposed joint-venture, project bid, or contract offer, or technical resource assessment.

The Value of Theoretical Knowledge

There are two forms of theoretical knowledge within the context of our discourse, they are:

A. **Explicit Theoretical Knowledge:** This is the knowledge that is part of the database of the organization, and it could be of different kinds such as market analysis and strategy data, product development information, intellectual property, or outcomes from R&D undertakings. These kinds of data and information are vital forms of business capital and are strategic to business success (Koudelková, 2015).

B. **Implicit Theoretical Knowledge:** This is a form of knowledge that comes through human agency. It is created within an organization and is a function of the quality of human capital inherent in the organization. Organizations that want to increase their innovative drive and push out lethargy and mediocrity must realize that they will only be successful if they create the right social environment (Isabel, 2011). To create the right social environment that promotes implicit knowledge, leaders should:

- Involve all employees or TEAM members in the innovation process and retain a consistent approach between all departments and TEAMs.
- Realize that it is important for employees to be encouraged to try out new ideas and methods.

Koudelková (2015) has noted that knowledge determines success or failure in business. Knowledge today is replacing land and capital as the major source of wealth in knowledge-driven economies. Mediocre leaders without the requisite theoretical competence are likely to struggle in the areas of innovation management, and where they try to innovate, they may not have the required skills to make the innovations profitable and successful. Experienced businessmen understand the relationship between technical knowledge and innovation, and it is why they are always on the lookout for the underlying information applicable to any innovation.

Today, businesses are faced with the challenge of employee motivation, knowledge transfer, and skill development, especially when they are looking to expand their operations, increase profit, or upgrade their workforce. Both explicit and implicit knowledge are referred to as knowledge assets, and they are intangible valuables that also help shape the success of an organization. They include technical know-how (i.e., hands-on skills), technical knowledge, product development information, production processes, intellectual property, etc. For instance, imitative entrepreneurs who do not invest in the acquisition of in-depth knowledge and skills but are only concerned about mere simulation of products or innovations will have challenges improving on such replications. This is bound to limit their ability to be competitive or retain whatever market share they gain after market entry. Mediocre leaders who do not appreciate these dynamics of theoretical knowledge cannot commit to it, and the result is that their organizations remain mediocre and cannot attain excellence.

Understanding Practical Knowledge

Schwenkler (2015) identifies practical knowledge as that knowledge that has become agential through the participatory involvement of a person or persons to formally cause something to happen tangibly. It is a unifying knowledge that is acted out as a bridge between an end and a means. Where knowledge is used as a function towards productive engagement beyond the mere perception of the individual(s) and tailored towards the achievement of specific ends, it is said to be practical knowledge. Mediocre leadership does not have this dimension to practical engagement because, in the first place, it is laid back in its cognitive engagements, and this, in turn, makes its reference to theoretical knowledge merely academic and cosmetic. The pivotal underpinning of practical knowledge is its ability to materialize in quantum terms, real-time outcomes, results, and effects, based on theoretical insights and understanding; where this is lacking, it is merely cosmetic.

Therefore, we find mediocre leaders often taking a cosmetic and shallow approach when it comes to practical terms or the practice of knowledge. They are scared to delve too deeply and lack the communicative abilities necessary to foster cognitive, interactive, and expressive understanding among TEAM members. This deficiency in communicative action that can bring about cognitive, interactive, and expressive engagement among TEAM members makes a mediocre leader fall short of the philosophical theory of practical knowledge—which is the production of action through these three processes (Guzman, 2009). The sociological school emphasizes the consequences of action as determined on the one hand by social structures (such as institutions, traditions, and rules), and on the other hand, by human agency. The sociological concept focuses on the ability of the leader to create systems, rules, and cultural behaviors that enhance practicality and how the leader puts knowledge into practice in order to achieve specific outcomes and effects. It is these two factors of social structures and social practices that are termed in practical knowledge parameters as objective and subjective dimensions, and they either enable or constrain the leader's realization of practical knowledge (Guzman, 2009).

Recognizing Mediocrity and Mediocre Thinking

Mediocre leaders lack the practical abilities, theoretical knowledge, and relevant experience necessary to give their leadership the edge, and as a result, they perform at a suboptimal level. It also happens that many such leaders do not recognize their incompetence or the inadequacies in their leadership. As Dunning, Johnson, and Kruger (2003) have observed in their double curse theory, individuals who are defective in certain respects are often unable to accurately evaluate themselves in relation to the skills in question because of their inferior metacognitive judgments. This theory flows from research-backed observations that show that in most cases, individuals rate their competence based on their own preconceived beliefs about their skills and which they, in turn, use as a yardstick to estimate how well they are doing or will do in an assigned role. At first, this top-down approach to self-assessment may seem justified, especially if they have acquired certain training, certifications, or some levels of experience in relation to skills they claim to possess; however, actual performance is a better yardstick to measure the competence level an individual possesses in relation to any skill. When competence is measured based on real results and outcomes, leaders are better able to assess their abilities and have an opportunity to identify gaps in their methods, skills, the quality of information they possess, and other associated factors.

In the context of mediocre leadership, the inferable hypothesis from this theory is that when leaders are able to distinguish optimal from suboptimal results, outcomes, approaches, or information, they then would be in a position to recognize their deficiencies or incompetence. This further implies that if mediocre leaders can develop the skills necessary to detect or distinguish excellence from mediocrity, they will invariably have the most vital take-off cognition needed to cure themselves of the latter and thus enhance their performance above the average scale. This would translate them from the recesses of mediocre leadership to becoming highly skilled, innovative, and effective leaders. In essence, excellence as a culture and as an outcome needs to be identifiable, and assessments must go beyond mere impressions or perceptions of the intellectual and social skills of individuals. This is vital in order to truly determine the level of skill set development in the specified areas that leaders need to prove themselves. This is one of the missing links in the decider on recruitments; i.e., employers tend to assume the competencies and abilities of prospects by mere perception, impressions from previous performance, or skill set claims, instead of an evaluation of pinpointed skills that the prospected employee should possess in order to fill the new role well. Later in this book, a definition and contextual analysis of excellence will be provided in order to juxtapose between a mediocre culture and one of excellence and to provide a workable template for leaders who wish to upgrade their self-evaluation to identifiable standards of excellence.

However, it is important to note that breaking the ceiling of mediocre leadership by developing competence will happen in stages, and we all start at the level of incompetence in the competence development process. Anyone who wants to develop their leadership abilities surely can; all they need is the will to grow and to challenge their traditional approach to thinking and learning.

The Peter Principle and the Stages of Competence

In delving further into the discussion on mediocre leadership and its associated vacuum in terms of intellectual and practical knowledge, it is important to clarify the point that mediocre leaders are not essentially "skill-less," neither are they always bereft of ideas, ambition, and knowledge. Though there are those who are less than inspirational, in many instances, even mediocre leaders have attained visibility and recognition through the consistency of their performance. The challenge is that sometimes mediocre performance is a result of being promoted to a point where one's competence level is below what is required in a new job role, even when performance in a previous position was well above average. This is what has now been termed as the Peter Principle.

Laurence J. Peter introduced the Peter Principle as a concept into corporate leadership and management analysis. It states that people in a hierarchical system tend to rise to their "level of incompetence." That is, employees are promoted based on their performance in previous jobs or assignments until they reach a level of promotion that is greater than their level of competence. The principle recognizes that superb skills and working knowledge on a level do not automatically translate to the same degree of competence on another level. This is why leaders and organizations alike have a responsibility to put in place well-designed mechanisms to ensure their leaders and employees are interacting with the latest industry information, developments, and skills upgrades. Leaders must sustain an appetite for learning, personal improvement, and skills upgrade. We learn through the conscious competence learning theory that there are generally four stages in the cycle of competence development. The four stages are depicted in the following diagram and further explained.

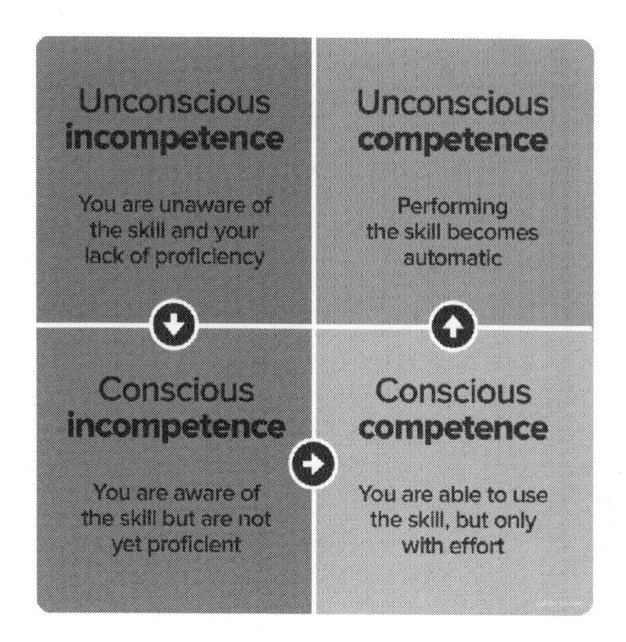

Fig 2.1 Four Stages of Competence Development. Adapted from Noel Burch's Diagram of the Conscious Competence Model, Gordon Training International (Adam, 2011)

(I) **Unconscious Incompetence:** At the stage of unconscious incompetence, the individual doesn't possess the "know-how" information/exposure required to deliver certain results or to deliver at a level of performance. It may also be difficult for the individual to initially recognize the deficit in the required skill. Where the individual is in denial or jettisons the importance of acquiring the relevant proficiency, the status quo of incompetence remains. But where the right value is ascribed to the acquisition of the new skill, there is a stimulus to learn, which advances the learner to the next stage. The level of stimulus in the learner determines how quickly the skill can be acquired or how long it would take to achieve both basic and advanced proficiency in the skill. Leaders who do not want to operate on an average scale could undertake a Training Needs Analysis/Assessment (TNA) to identify specific areas where they are strong or weak. A TNA will help answer questions like:

- "In what areas do I need training?"
- "Why do I need to acquire this skill, knowledge, or experience?"
- "How do I undertake this training?"

(II) **Conscious Incompetence:** At this stage of competence development, the individual is incompetent and aware of this deficit. It is also called the stage of awareness. It is a strategic transition phase in skill acquisition and development because the consciousness of gaps in information, experience, or practical skills, provides a better self-assessment and positions the individual to address the deficits. This could also determine the level of stimulus motivation that the individual could show in the learning process. Mediocre leaders who are unconscious of their incompetence have no internal or external stimulus to alter the status quo; however, the consciousness of their incompetence in itself may not be a sufficient basis for them to engage in the skill acquisition process if they don't recognize the value. In other circumstances, their reactions could be hostile, irrational, or withdrawn. Where their positions are threatened, they often give some form of dutiful response as a form of self-preservation, but this caps their level of engagement, creativity, and resourceful abilities at a minimal level and doesn't allow them to maximize their potentials.

Value recognition for the acquisition of a new skill or area of proficiency is a vital nexus towards attaining the right mindset (cognition), culture, and redefining the standards of performance. At this level of learning, it is normal to accommodate mistakes as an integral part of the learning process.

(III) **Conscious Competence:** At this level of competence, the individual has developed or acquired some degree of "know-how," insight, and experience, but there is a required degree of exertion and concentration that comes with demonstrating the said skill or knowledge. At this level of performance, conscious efforts are made to break down the execution and implementation of ideas and procedures into manageable steps while applying the new skill. The consciousness of competence at this point stems from a deliberate effort and initiative already taken to acquire a skill, develop some form of proficiency, or acquire knowledge, after which the learner puts to practice what has been learned. It is based on the outcomes and results at this level that employers, prospective, and existing leaders should measure how much they are able to demonstrate specific skills and abilities in practical terms. This phase of competence development is both a demonstration and assessment stage, and the leader is reinforcing the skills that have been learned. Taking up volunteer positions that will help sharpen their new skills is one way that individuals can continually exercise themselves and reinforce their learning. This will help increase their proficiency levels under less stringent yet professionally relevant circumstances and environment.

At this stage of competence development, mediocre leaders who maintain a stiff disposition are not able to display what we call Job Crafting. This is a skill often used by enterprising leaders who utilize opportunities and avenues on the job to adjust or influence operations to reflect their unique skill set in order to enhance performance. They deploy their skills and areas of strength in a manner that enhances the performance of the department or the position they occupy, such that the activities take on an outlook that better fits into the skill set of the leader. The goal of the leader here is to use innovation and the underlying skill set to enhance performance while retaining other valuable tools and resources hitherto in place.

(IV) **Unconscious Competence:** This is the stage of mastery. Unfortunately, mediocre leaders never get to this stage in relation to excellence. There is no gainsaying that everyone has a tendency to be very good at something —even if it is mastering the art of demoralizing people or being a clog in the wheel of change, but unconscious competence comes from consistently repeating a cycle of behavior, practice, or skill until it becomes second nature. Oftentimes, mediocre leaders who wish to change their thinking and the outcomes they get will find that they must go through a de-programming from their previous pattern of thinking or initial leadership approach. Both excellence and mediocrity can become second nature depending on which of them is consistently reinforced; therefore, the dominant culture in an organization is dependent on which of the two value systems is reinforced through practice.

Inadequacy in Developmental Challenges and Experience

Mediocre leadership can also be a product of limited exposure in terms of developmental challenges and experiences. The developmental value of professional and leadership experience is well noted, especially when leaders have been exposed to real-time challenges that develop their problem-solving responses and abilities (DeRue and Wellman, 2009). When prospective candidates for leadership positions have not been tested in challenging situations that have tried their capabilities, they are less likely to have well-toned psychological muscles that prepare them for tough challenges ahead. Experience plays a crucial role in leadership because of the privilege of hindsight, the tact, and unique insights that it bestows on leaders who have had the privilege of acquiring such experience. Experiential learning theories have posited that effective learning occurs when individuals engage in challenging experiences and have the privilege of reflecting on the responses to those challenges or the outcomes of the said challenges. More so, these challenges increase the cognitive involvement of the individual and can help to sharpen their leadership skills.

It is important to strike a balance in the developmental value that facing challenges provide leaders, especially because adult learning theories suggest that the uncertainties of success and excellent performance due to overly challenging situations can become significantly overwhelming that it slows down the learning process or compromises the development of the leader. This doesn't in any way compromise the developmental value of challenges; nevertheless, these challenging experiences may reach a point of diminishing returns for a leader who has faced a certain threshold at which point the performance level begins to decline (DeRue and Wellman, 2009). Altogether, the downside to this is that mediocre leaders, by their nature, evade and avoid tackling problems and difficult situations. They are peeved, evasive, or confused when they have to deal with intricate situations, and they are inclined to do everything to avoid such complex realities. This, in turn, limits their problem-solving capabilities, reduces their exposure to experiential knowledge, and denies them vital professional or leadership experiences. Two important considerations stand out in harnessing and optimizing the value of experience:

1. **Creating opportunities for developmental experiences:** Although the relationship between challenges and leadership skill development may be a positive one, it is important to emphasize that it isn't a straightforward linear relationship or effect (DeRue and Wellman, 2009).

Characteristically, professional or work-related engagements that are not rich in developmental experiences or challenges are less likely to stimulate the intelligence and cognitive energies of leaders in problem-solving; but there is also the risk of inducing cognitive overload in leaders through overwhelming tasks, which could weaken their morale and lead to a decline in their productivity. However, it is important to state that some form of developmental challenge is necessary to "activate" an individual's cognitive abilities and innate potentials for leadership development; what matters is that leaders who have been exposed to tasking and strenuous activities are allowed to rejuvenate and not overloaded to their breaking points. Captured in the table below is an illustration of five areas through which developmental challenges can help a promising employee develop leadership abilities and acquire relevant experience.

Type of Developmental Challenge	Description	Examples
Undertaking unfamiliar responsibilities	Assigned to handle novel responsibilities and deliver on them.	An employee experiencing a major change in his/her work, involving new forms of responsibilities and tasks.
Creating change	A need to create and facilitate change, for instance, in the mode of doing business, in employee behavior, or in TEAM culture. It could also include resolving a preexisting organizational problem.	Managing a new product launch, leading business or assets acquisitions, managing subordinate performance problems, or addressing inherited morale problems within the organization.

Type of Developmental Challenge	Description	Examples
Undertaking high levels of responsibility	To lead major initiatives or interventions that are highly important to the organization and entail multiple functions, TEAMs, projects, or products/services.	▪ Securing funding for a new significant acquisition. ▪ Negotiating a major deal with a major business partner or customer. ▪ Assuming new responsibilities for a nationwide or regional initiative.
Working across boundaries	Influencing and managing people or processes in other units or departments where one has no direct authority.	▪ Convincing senior management to ratify a proposal. ▪ Managing key interactions with a major project partner in a joint venture operation. ▪ Liaising and negotiating with a labor union.
Managing diversity	Coordinating people from different cultures, gender, racial, ethnic, or professional backgrounds.	▪ Leading a unit or TEAM of employees dispersed across a country, region, or different continents. ▪ Coordinating a TEAM with extensive gender and racial backgrounds. ▪ Coordinating a project involving professionals from diverse fields.

Table 2.1 Five Areas of Developmental Challenges that Strengthen Leadership. Adapted from De Rue and Wellman (2009)

2. **Mitigating the diminishing effects of overwhelming challenges:** When leaders deal with a barrage of situations, they could show signs of stress due to cognitive overload. Identified below are two mitigating factors that could help offset the diminishing effects of developmental experiences, they are:

   i. **Learning Orientation:** This can be done by emphasizing the value of learning and re-construing failures and mistakes on the job as feedback and opportunities for learning instead of seeing them as performance problems. There is a need to help leaders who make honest mistakes or who fail on a project despite well-thought-out and executed plans to understand that mistakes and failures are part of growth. This will help curtail the disillusionment, sense of defeat, or discouragement they feel. This will also curb the diminishing effect of seemingly overwhelming challenges as leaders begin to see those challenges from a different lens.

   ii. **Feedback Availability:** The second mitigating factor is the context in which the employee works in terms of access to feedback. When employees have access to feedback in relation to initiatives and responsibilities discharged in the course of their work, the availability of feedback provides a veritable platform for the employees to assess the appropriateness of the approach and correctness of behavior in the pursuit of set goals. This will help curtail uncertainties that are associated with challenging work experiences.

Flowing from the above, developmental challenges play an essential role in experience-based leadership development (Ohlott, 2004). Theoretical, practical, and experiential knowledge are vital to leadership success.

CHAPTER THREE

INEFFECTIVE COMMUNICATION SKILLS

"To effectively communicate, we must realize that we are all different in the way we perceive the world and use this understanding as a guide to our communication with others."
—Anthony Robbins

Case Study: The Charge of the Light Brigade, 1854

Although what seemed to launch the Crimean War in 1854 has probably been forgotten in collective memory, it was a tragic time in history. In 1854, the conflict erupted with the Russian Empire on one side, and on the other side, the Brits, the French, the Kingdom of Sardinia, and the Ottoman Empire. The central dispute was on which side would have a dominant influence in the declining Ottoman Empire. The war's major battleground was in the Russian Crimean Peninsula, where the war got its name. In the fall of 1854, British and French forces landed in Crimea to attack Russia's naval base at Sevastopol and thereby weakened its naval presence in the Black Sea.

While the war seems to now be only a dim recollection, there is a valorously tragic incident that occurred during the campaign: the headlong cavalry charge of the British Light Brigade into the murderous Russian fire. This action was immortalized by Alfred Lord Tennyson's poem "The Charge of the Light Brigade." The second and third verses captured the tragedy of what happened, depicting how dangerous miscommunication or ineffective communication can be:

II

"Forward, the Light Brigade!"

Was there a man dismayed?

Not though the soldier knew

Someone had blundered.

Theirs not to make reply,

Theirs not to reason why,

Theirs but to do and die.

Into the valley of Death

Rode the six hundred.

III

Cannon to right of them,

Cannon to left of them,

Cannon in front of them

Volleyed and thundered;

Stormed at with shot and shell,

Boldly they rode and well,

Into the jaws of Death,

Into the mouth of hell

Rode the six hundred.

The Charge of the Light Brigade occurred during a battle near Balaclava on October 25, 1854. As a result of a miscommunication of orders, the Light Brigade of roughly 600 horsemen started a headlong charge into a treeless valley to capture some Russian field artillery at its end. Lord Raglan's intention for the original order was to send the Light Brigade to prevent the Russians from taking away the captured guns from overrun Turkish positions. However, there was miscommunication in the chain of command; the Light Brigade was instead sent on a frontal assault against a different artillery battery, one well-prepared with excellent fields of defensive fire. Unknown to them, the valley was ringed on three sides by about 20 battalions of Russian infantry and artillery.

The result was overwhelmingly tragic. About 278 of the Light Brigade were killed or wounded. In retrospect of the charge, a French Marshall said: "It is magnificent, but it is not war. It is madness." When the news of it reached London, it led to a national scandal that inspired Tennyson to pen his poem.

Based on historical accounts, when the original order was relayed to the troops, it lacked insight into the bigger picture of their strategy. Also, it was one of those miscommunications that became so convoluted that no one knew precisely who gave what orders and why. Years after that war, some of the higher-ups kept pointing fingers and absolving themselves of responsibility.

While we may not be going into battle on horsebacks, this kind of miscommunication occurs within TEAMs and companies regularly, especially bigger companies where message origination gets lost in the shuffle, and no one seems to be able to clarify the strategy. Miscommunication between TEAM members probably does not lead to catastrophes like the one of war, but they can harm business performance.

Leaders who do not possess a quality build but who only flaunt titles and positions as status symbols, opportunities to get higher paychecks, or as the next big thing they need in their career trajectory are often pedestrian in their approach, and this makes them ineffective communicators. This is because apart from their streamlined communication focus on tasks and processes as a way of driving subordinates to deliver and proving their worth; they are not endowed with other vital qualities such as the tact, passion, and compassion they need to under guard their communication at apposite times. Frequent, direct, and clear communication is important in any effective leadership framework, and only resourceful leaders know how to invigorate their TEAM members and subordinates with the vision and purpose of their jobs. They are thus able to help employees appreciate the importance of their tasks in accomplishing the broad, immediate, and day-to-day goals of the organization.

Apart from this deficiency in the ability to inspire and motivate the TEAM, and the somewhat simplistic preoccupation with tasks and processes, analysts agree that mediocre leaders who aren't adept at communication feel insecure, avoid engagement, and feel the need to protect their authority from being undermined by subordinates. They could also become confused, emotionally unstable, hostile, or authoritarian (Conner, 2011; Llopis, 2015). Conner (2011) noted that an atmosphere of misunderstanding, confusion/anger, blaming, alienation, and hostility are the prevalent elements that result from ineffective communication within a group of people working together.

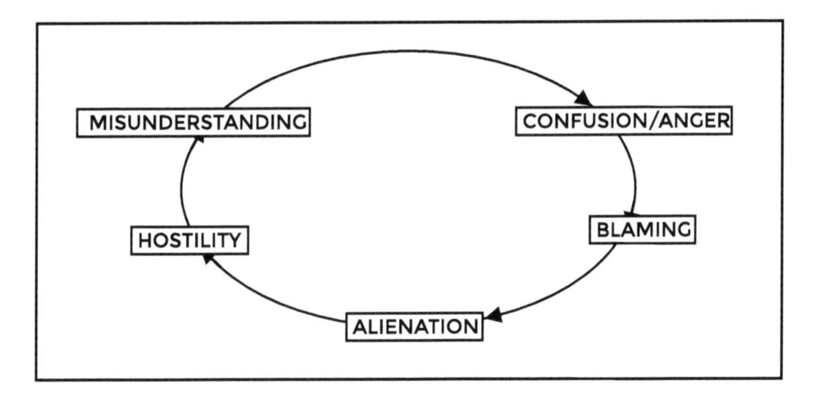

Fig 3.1 Resultant Effects of Ineffective Communication (Source: Conner, 2011)

In the same way that ineffective communication affects the climate within a flat group, so also does it affect the climate in a hierarchical organization. One difference that might be readily observed is that due to power asymmetry, the hierarchical leader/superior may be able to vent his anger, alienate himself from complex situations, and blame others when things go wrong, while subordinates are forced to submissively put up with it. These subordinates who are on the receiving cannot direct their frustrations at their superiors but are likely to transfer the aggression to colleagues and customers while they grapple with the alienation, hostilities, misunderstanding, confusion, and blame game.

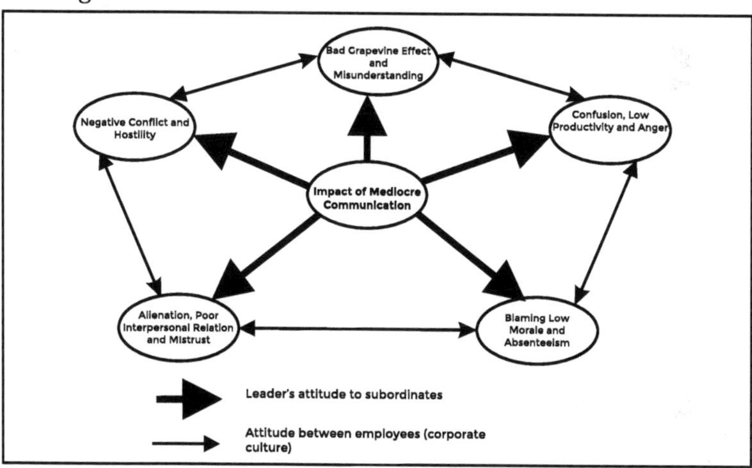

Fig 3.2 A Depiction of the Organizational Impact of Ineffective Communication Skills

Employees are also not able to give their best because ineffective communication channels hinder information flow, and since no one wants to be on the spot or feel embarrassed due to a lack of information, it breeds all kinds of negative effects. Attributes like employee distrust, low morale, frequent absenteeism at emergency meetings (caused by lack of information), poor interpersonal interactions all become entrenched in the organization (Grossman, 2020). This scenario leads to frequent conflict. These things also happen because the leader hasn't clearly defined the roles of

TEAM members, timelines aren't clearly stated, gossips and blaming are rife, and there is poor coordination between units and departments working on the same project (McQuerrey, 2019). Since employees and subordinates aren't able to give their best in such circumstances, the productivity level both in the individual and corporate contexts will also be low. Employees who are not clear on expectations and requirements cannot carry out their jobs effectively and efficiently (Tankersley, 2015).

Mediocre Leaders and the Communication Conundrum

One of the essential qualities for professional success and organizational performance is the ability to communicate well, whether in verbal or non-verbal form (Malik & Girdhar, 2018; Luthra & Dahiya, 2015; De la Fuente, 2016). Communication, which has been defined as the process of understanding and sharing meaning, is indispensable to creating interactions and sharing information within an organization (Pearson & Nelson, 2000). This definition further suggests that communication is a process, and it involves the cognitive exercise of understanding what is communicated and decoding what is actually meant. An excellent communicator is, therefore, anyone who can share information in a meaningful way that is understood among participants in the exchange. This is where leaders with mediocre skills often stumble, i.e., they struggle to understand or ensure clarity of intent and meaning in their communication and thus create communication problems that can impede the under-standing of those they lead. This increases the incidence of confusion and derails the productivity of their workforce.

Highlighted in the diagram below are some of the attributes of mediocre communication skills that average leaders may exhibit and even impose on the organization due to the inherent defects in their ability to interact with their subordinates, TEAM members, colleagues, or even superiors.

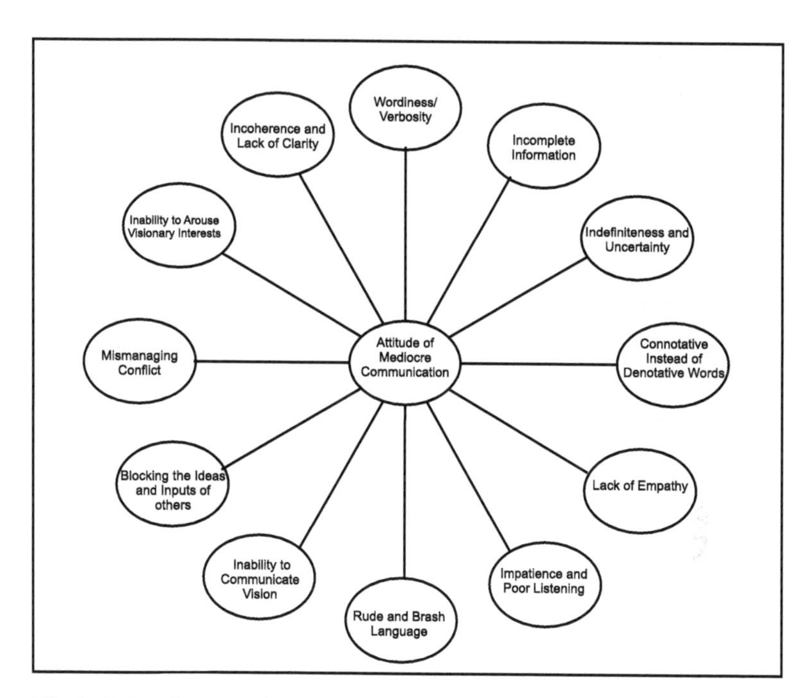

Fig 3.3 Twelve Attributes of Mediocre Communication Skills in Leadership

1. **Inability to communicate vision:** Experts have identified vision casting or "visioning" as an essential competence required of leadership (Martin, 2011; Kouzes & Posner, 2009). Visioning is one of the distinctive marks that separate leaders from managers in the closer sense of distinction between them. In elucidating on the marks of transformational leadership at the close of the 20th Century, Bass (1990) argued against the transactional nature of communication known to transactional leadership, advocating the superior traits of transformational leadership, which lie in the ability to broaden and elevate the interests of employees beyond their personal interests and pecuniary gains. This brings them to the more inspirational level of inculcating the vision, mission, and objectives of the organization or group as the motivating drive for their commitment. Also, this demands

that strong leaders are charismatic and inspiring in a way that stimulates their employees intellectually and meets their need for motivation.

One of the most crucial responsibilities of leadership is the ability to communicate a vision and build a compelling case for the vision in order to align the focus and efforts of employees. It is simply impracticable to lead a group of people to succeed if they do not know what the success point is. The challenge, however, is that imprinting a vision on the minds of others and getting them to buy into it requires a constellation of other efforts. It is in these other areas that mediocre leaders struggle. Maxwell (2011) observes that the following steps are crucial to helping a leader communicate the vision of the organization:

- **Connecting with them relationally:** Leaders need to project that they care and find good grounds through which they can connect with their TEAM. People buy into the leader first before they buy into the vision, which is why leaders need to first make an impression that wins over the people's attention and gains their respect. Mediocre leaders struggle here because they do not know how to connect with people.

- **Simplifying the message:** What you say as a leader is important, but it is also important how you say it. Make the content and presentation of your message both simple and memorable enough so that it can stick and people can follow. Leaders who cannot simplify their message and make it something that people can remember will have difficulty maximizing their potentials and that of their TEAM.

- **Embodying the vision:** Be a living example of what the vision is about. Let your employees and subordinates be able to always look at you in order to realign with or reinforce their understanding of the vision. The passion of the leader creates compelling imagery that people can closely relate with, and imagery is a powerful tool to inspire people's responses and clarify their thoughts on a subject. This is why telling stories get more attention than spewing bare facts. Mediocre leadership is often passionless and mechanical, and therefore it doesn't achieve exceptional results! Help your people see what you are saying through your passion.

- **Prioritizing influencers:** For a vision to take root in an organization, it is important that significant people in the links understand the vision. This is why even though great leaders make an effort to imprint the vision on the hearts and minds of their TEAM in general, they also recognize the strategic value of influencers across the organization and get them to buy into the vision. This requires talking to key decision-makers one-on-one, addressing concerns, answering their questions, getting vital information from them, and convincing them. Once you get the buy-in of strategic influencers and leaders in the ranks, they will sell the vision to other members of the organization they have influence over and help you implement the vision. Average leaders often have an unhealthy sense of rivalry, pride, and reluctance that hedges them in and prevents them from relating proactively with the people they need to achieve outstanding results.

- **Honoring the process:** Average leaders expect that after discussing the vision with the people and hammering on its importance, that is where it ends; well, they are dead wrong! Leadership is an engaging process, and so is vision casting. Skillful leaders know that they must utilize every opportunity they get to reinforce the vision in the minds of those they lead.

They take advantage of every moment they get to re-enact the vision in the minds of the people while they ensure to sustain the TEAM's morale, especially in difficult times. The vision must be constantly emphasized; otherwise, it would soon take the backseat and fade into oblivion.

- **Calling people to action:** Excellent leaders know that they need to enlist people in an actionable strategy to succeed. They are not out to just excite their employees or TEAM members but to rouse them into definite action in line with the picture that the vision inspires and projects in their minds. Taking action is vital to success. Leaders who talk a lot and plan a lot but take no action soon see their TEAMs deteriorate.

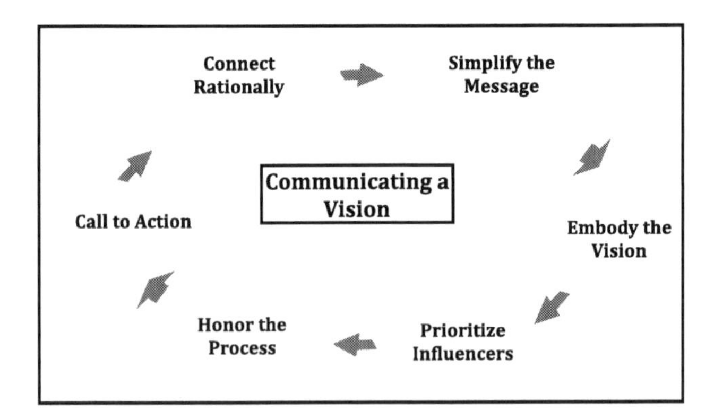

Fig 3.4 Maxwell's Steps to Communicating a Vision

2. **Incoherence and lack of clarity:** The most important quality of a good communicator is clarity and coherence in passing across information. Mediocre leaders are seldom able to express their intents in a clear and unambiguous manner so that the receiver can understand what is being communicated and respond accordingly. This may not mean that the mediocre leader doesn't have

a strong vocabulary; in fact, in many cases, such leaders may be expressive, but they are not sensitive enough to use precise, concrete, and familiar words that their audience can interpret correctly. They instead want to put up an impressive showing to their subordinates and miss the point of communication. In other instances, the sentences could be unduly long, grammatically incoherent, and confusing. Communication needs to be concrete, clear, and coherent for it to be meaningful.

3. **Wordiness or verbosity:** When a leader is not able to pass across the message in a concise and brief manner, but gives in to the merry-go-round manner of speaking, and also includes irrelevant information that gives the receiver of the information a hard time in discerning the most important details, such communication is verbose and ineffective. Leaders should be able to distill the most relevant information that they want to pass across and communicate in as few words as possible. This way, they can sustain the interest of the receiver, pinpoint the most important details, and save time. Using easy-to-understand words and avoiding unnecessary repetitions are also vital aspects of effective communication within the leadership and organizational context.

4. **Incomplete information:** When information that should be disseminated at once is handed down in incomplete doses, it can make communication laborious. Both the giver and receiver should be diligent in assessing what the relevant facts are regarding the information in question and ensure to deliver them in holistic terms. When subordinates always have to get clarification from their boss on a given piece of information or assigned tasks, it leads to inefficiency. Inefficiency is when productivity is not maximized due to excessive drain on time and resources in the pursuit of stated goals and objectives. Therefore, it is important that communication provides an avenue to

gain all available and relevant information needed to execute a task.

5. **Indefiniteness and uncertainty:** Mediocre leaders can sometimes get things rowdy and base their communication on guesses, incorrect facts, vague ideas that they do not have a good understanding of, and spontaneous thoughts without solid footing. This creates situations of uncertainty, doubts, and inconclusiveness. It can also create an atmosphere in which employees are always second-guessing and suspicious of the thoroughness of decisions.

6. **Connotative instead of denotative Words:** Leaders who are well skilled in communication are mindful of how they use connotative words and would rather prefer to use words that are denotative. Denotative meanings refer to the actual ideas or objects being referred to instead of the various ideas and meaning that connotative communication may suggest. This reduces incidences of mistaken understanding and ambiguity. For instance, the word "health practitioner" has a connotative quality because it could refer to anyone who practices as a professional in the health sector; however, using the word "pharmacist" streamlines the communication to a health practitioner who works in a pharmacy and makes this denotative. A connotation is the use of a word in a context that is different from its literal dictionary meaning, such as: "When a person becomes blue due to loss of a loved one, the company makes an exception on its leave policy." The word "blue" by its literal dictionary meaning is a color, but in this context, it connotes sadness or grief. Using such connotative language is not advisable in practical business or formal relations.

7. **Lack of empathy:** Mediocre leaders do not show empathy, either because they are alienated from their people or because they see it as a sign of weakness. Communication is effective when the sender of the information is able to

take into consideration the inclinations, feelings, expectations, and reactions of the receiver of the information and accord the necessary sense of humanity as it applies to the situation. Maintaining a positive and pleasant behavior that is reflected through communication and identifying the reasonable limits of what can be demanded from subordinates and members of the TEAM will help enhance the communicative abilities of a leader. This social intelligence gives a leader the ability to connect with people at a personal level, even within the formal nature of the work environment, without compromising professional ethics.

8. **Impatience and poor listening:** Mediocre leaders do not have the patience and culture of listening attentively; instead, they are often in a hurry to respond and talk back. They only listen for as long as it takes them to react or talk back, not necessarily to pay attention to what they are told and to process it before giving their response. This is more common with an oral exchange. However, even though written communication provides such leaders a greater opportunity to pay attention to what the sender is saying, their impatience many times still catches up with them. Many of these leaders either miss out on valuable details that are written legibly in the document or read their preconceived notions into the content of the document. Good communicators are good listeners, and they also take time to think, process the information they have received, and then give a proper response.

9. **Rude and brash language:** Mediocre leaders who have developed a sense of entitlement, who are under pressure, or feel threatened, are prone to brash and rude behavior. Their communication could be laced with threats, harsh language, and devoid of courtesy. Arrogance and ill-temper are not excusable attitudes, and outstanding leaders know this because they have that much

emotional intelligence to address issues without getting into a fit. They know when to be frank without losing the refinement of courtesy or deflating the professionalism and grace that should accompany the status of the positions they occupy. Discerning leaders are thoughtful, appreciative of dissent, and are engaging in their interactions with subordinates, colleagues, or superiors alike. They know how to be firm, use language skillfully, and have a sense of decency that makes them show genuine respect for people, especially those they interact with at work.

10. **Inability to arouse interest through visionary and innovative communication:** Leaders performing at the mediocre level will have a hard time inspiring the interest and motivation of those they lead from a visionary standpoint. It is visionary leaders who have the spark of the organization's vision, are full of positive energy, and can connect to the hearts and minds of their employees that are able to communicate the vision, values, and objectives of the organization in a manner that catches on in the mind of the employees. Slight movements—not excessive movements which could be distracting—and cheerfulness while speaking or conversing could also help to make the exchange lively. This way, enthusiastic leaders are able to rub off their conviction, passion, and enthusiasm on their subordinates and thus inspire them to take on the tasks with enthusiasm, develop themselves, and grow their career on the job.

Unlike mediocre leaders, they are conscious of possible filters and barriers to communication and do everything to mitigate or curb them. In oral communication, they ensure that their voice quality and speech modulation are done in such a manner as to alternate stressed and unstressed sounds, and this makes the message lively. If the communication will be in writing, then it is vital to consider the following (MTD Training, 2010):

- Have subject lines, which are like headlines giving receivers pointers to what is contained in the information.
- Put the main point first, i.e., state the reason for writing immediately.
- Know your audience and fine-tune the message to meet the peculiarities of the particular or different segments of the audience you are addressing.
- Organize your communication in such a manner that the call to action is clear, specific, and unambiguous. Where there are several calls to action that are unrelated, you might want to consider writing different letters, emails or circulars, so that employees can respond to each differently and note the distinctions in the communications more easily.

11. **Blocking the inputs and ideas of others:** Leaders who see communication as one-way traffic that largely emanates from them as orders and instructions to subordinates do not encourage the flow of ideas and constructive opinions of employees and members of their TEAM. This leads to a culture of silence, stifles knowledge and information sharing, and cuts off innovative thinking and the chances of fresh ideas that could lead to new opportunities for growth and expansion. Communication is the nerve of knowledge and information sharing, and great leaders know that if they want to remain on the cutting edge of the latest developments and information in the market, they need to encourage a culture of open communication, flexibility, and effective communication channels within the organization. Leaders should ensure that in group or TEAM conversations, one or two people

are not allowed to dominate the conversations—including the leader—instead, a diversity of inputs from other members of the TEAM should be allowed.

This further underscores the importance of leaders being good listeners and that they do not just breeze through situations in order to arrive at quick decisions. The valuable insights, constructive criticisms, and alternative options proffered by members of the TEAM could lead to better decisions even in urgent situations. When leaders engage a pool of resourceful people in the decision-making process, they are likely to make better informed and qualitative decisions. This does not erode their place in the scheme of things but rather enhances their leadership and the outcomes they get. However, mediocre leaders are often preoccupied with their limited perspectives, insecurities, and poor interpersonal inclinations and soon find themselves coercing their subordinates and other members of the TEAM into silence. This makes them deny the organization the opportunity of otherwise valuable insights, fresh ideas, and innovative thinking.

Leaders who are able to manage differences in opinions and skillfully deal with the complexities that come with aggregating diverse views also realize that divergence in opinions could be a result of differences in judgmental skills and sources of information, and this gives TEAM members an opportunity to enhance their own views from the variety of information processed, and make their opinions more objective (Bradley, 2007).

12. **Mismanaging conflict:** Mediocre leaders often view conflict from a narrow and negative sense and would rather prevent its occurrence than benefit from it. But great leaders know that when communication is open and there is a healthy sense of duty and contribution from employees, there is bound to be conflict of ideas, perspectives, or opinions. The role of the leader is to help

employees turn away from taking these brainstorming sessions personally and keep their focus on what is best for the company or organization. It takes excellent communication and interpersonal skills to defuse conflict situations and keep employees intellectually engaged and vibrant. Conflict situations do not have to become toxic, as long as they remain discussions about the most viable course of action and do not degenerate into fits of unhealthy rivalry, personal vendetta, and abuse of privilege. Good communicators avoid using language that is unhealthy, unprofessional, and inflammatory. They instead communicate their dissent or difference of opinion with candor, a sense of TEAMwork, and professionalism. An essential part of excellent TEAM leadership is conflict management (Levi, 2017).

Good communicators have the clarity of mind needed to make their oral messages and even written pieces clear, concrete, and effective. They first articulate what they want to say, straighten out all points and facts that need to be raised, and clarify what they want to emphasize before they engage in any form of communication. They speak in straightforward language that is simple to understand and leave no room for confusion, ambiguity, or misunderstanding. This is why they do a lot of groundwork to ensure precision and concretization of their message. When good communicators engage others, they exude energy, healthy self-esteem, and they are not self-absorbed, withdrawn, or touchy.

Average leaders become unsure of themselves when they deal with sophisticated or complex situations and can become evasive, withdrawn, touchy, or broken down, and this reflects in their disposition and body language (Seiter 2015; Maxfield & Hale, 2018; Malik & Girdhar, 2018). On the other hand, good communicators exhibit self-confidence, which shows in their body language, and they have an enthusiastic disposition and positive attitude towards life (Malik & Girdhar, 2018).

Ten Communication Functions and Why you Can't Afford Mediocrity

Leaders will need to harness the power of communication in order to be successful both in the external and internal contexts of their organizations. Every organization must interact with its immediate external environment, whether in its product marketing efforts, in building its corporate image, or in carrying out its objects—and all of these involve communication. In the same vein, this also applies to its internal environment. Captured below are some of the vital functions of communication that a leader must appreciate.

1. **The image-making and public relations function:** Communication skills and plans are vital to building the image of an organization. Leaders are image-makers of their organizations by virtue of the positions they occupy. They will often find themselves taking vital initiatives to interact with their market or target audience in pursuit of their objectives or make several statements to the press, stakeholders, and the public where the need arises. Poor or inadequate communication skills can blur the image and perception of an organization in the public eye and strengthen its competitors who may be doing better at communication. Organizations need to sustain a consistent image to build a reputation, gain competitive advantages, increase sales, and enjoy better relations with investors, opinion leaders, and the community. Scholars in public relations and marketing agree that corporate image is a result of the net impressions formed about an organization in the minds of the public, based on the activities of the communicators of its corporate identity (Karaosmanoglu & Melewar, 2006).

Corporate communication includes communication in different formats, the organizational capability to hatch comprehensive communication plans, and organizing communication tools and channels. It includes branding items, promotional materials, managers' communication at public events, media briefings, public relations, executive speeches, annual reports, and other unplanned communications at the interpersonal, intermediary (e.g., through media channels), and intrapersonal levels. Intrapersonal opinions could come from previously-stored experiences that customers have had in relation to an organization, its product, or its service. The quality of customers' communication experience with a representative or spokesperson of an organization can go a long way to influence the decisions of these customers. The combined sensitivity of planned and unplanned communication, especially in competitive environments, is one reason why mediocre levels of communication skills should not be tolerated in leadership.

2. **The information function:** Communication, in general, is the process by which information, thoughts, opinions, facts, ideas, messages, emotions, or some form of understanding is transmitted from one person, place or thing, to another person, place, or thing (NIAEM, 2012). At the information level, it helps to bring awareness and knowledge to individuals on the necessary guidance and inputs that they need to perform their tasks or duties. Therefore, it is important that communication is effective in order to ascertain that employees are properly informed and guided on their various tasks. Without proper information flow, work processes will suffer, and effectiveness will be affected.

3. **The instructive function:** This is when communication serves as a medium of formally instructing employees on their obligations or assignments and providing them with

the guidelines and internal protocols they need to take cognizance of in order to discharge their duties. It is also called the command or control function of communication and is a vital link to directing the affairs of employees and subordinates. The command function of language holds strategic importance in organizational communication, and leaders need to know how to skillfully apply this function for effectiveness.

4. **The persuasion and influence function:** This is a function of communication that leaders need to be able to stimulate and motivate their TEAM to reach the zenith of their potentials, helping them to see how their tasks are beneficial to the organization's goals and to their individual careers. Communication can also be a tool for leaders to grow their influence within the organization and thus get their TEAM and employees to be more involved in helping the leader achieve his agenda at specific times or phases of the organization. When employees are not persuaded or positively influenced, they do not go the extra mile. Leaders who want to succeed big need to be aware that there is an influence function of communication, and they need to play their cards well to utilize it. Excellent leaders know that the communication process could use written messages, spoken words, and gestures (such as cues, signals, facial expressions, spatial relationships, or even silence). Knowing what form of communication is most appropriate requires social observation and intelligence.

5. **The integrative function:** This aspect of communication is where the leader recognizes the need to ensure that the efforts and activities of employees complement the goals and objectives of the organization. This means that information, ideas, and suggestions by leaders and subordinates alike must be passed in such a way that it doesn't lead people to undertake activities that will cause

them to detract from the core assignments and the short and long-term goals of the organization. Communication must help to emphasize and harmonize the various activities so that employees can make sense of them in relation to the core objects of the organization.

6. **The planning function:** Without effective communication, planning is not possible. Planning is an essential function in management and leadership. More importantly, the quality of communication abilities that a leader exhibit determines how well planning will go. Organizations or departments that observe a constant repetition of disorganized or sloppy planning most likely suffer from ineffective or mediocre leadership. To successfully plan and organize, leaders should allow for and encourage a free flow of communication both upward and downward in the organizational hierarchy, as well as between departments and colleagues.

7. **The project management function:** When leaders, such as project managers, have to coordinate with other TEAMs to execute specific projects within specific timelines, communication management skills also become essential. Mediocre leaders should not be trusted with project management functions due to the complexities that could be involved and the limited room for failure. In a project context, vital to project success is drafting a project communication plan that highlights how information will be communicated across each level of the project TEAM and to stakeholders. Project TEAMs could sometimes be large, which is why communication should be divided into two levels to simplify the process, i.e.:

   - High-level communications which occur at strategic levels between the project manager and executives, sponsors, executive bodies, stakeholders, media, etc.

- Low-level communications which occur in the practical day-to-day activities between routine TEAM members of the project as they carry out their designated tasks.

It is generally advisable to divide TEAMs into units of five people (communication stage) or, at most, units of seven people (scaling stage) in order to ensure effectiveness (Pasqualis, 2017). However, where the project TEAM is necessarily large, it is better to operate through the Team of Leads Level (TOLL) in which technical leaders of similar TEAMs form a TEAM to represent the collective and various interests of their units within the larger network. For example, if a construction site involves five active sections being run concurrently, those working on the exterior structures in each of the sections can be collected in a TEAM, those working on the interior fittings in each of the sections can be collected into another TEAM, while the leaders of the two TEAMs could then be part of a central coordination TEAM headed by the project manager (see diagram below).

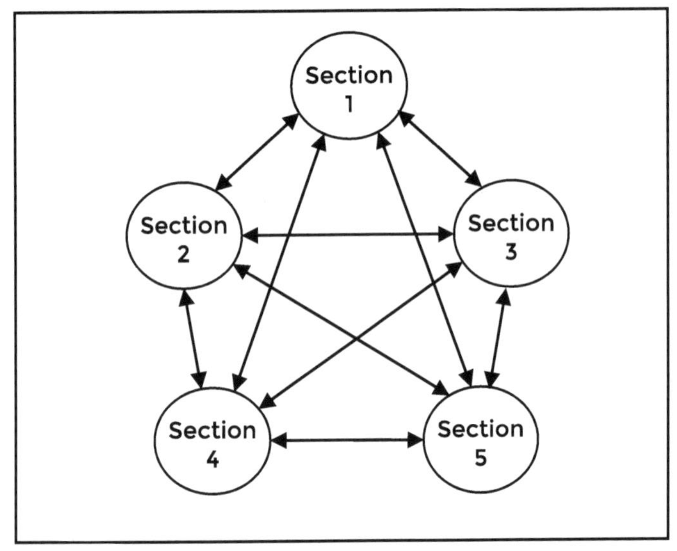

Fig 3.5 Exterior Construction Unit

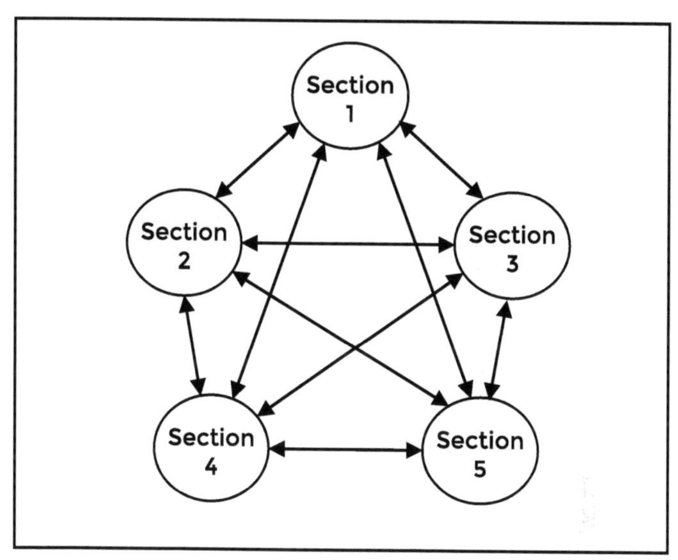

Fig 3.6 Interior Construction Unit

In the diagrams above, each of the five sections of the construction site has a leader under exterior construction and under interior construction. These leaders can interact at the sectional level under the two different units. But at the central level depicted in the diagram that follows below, all leaders under exterior construction then form a unit, while those under interior construction form another unit to interact at a central level with the project manager (PM).

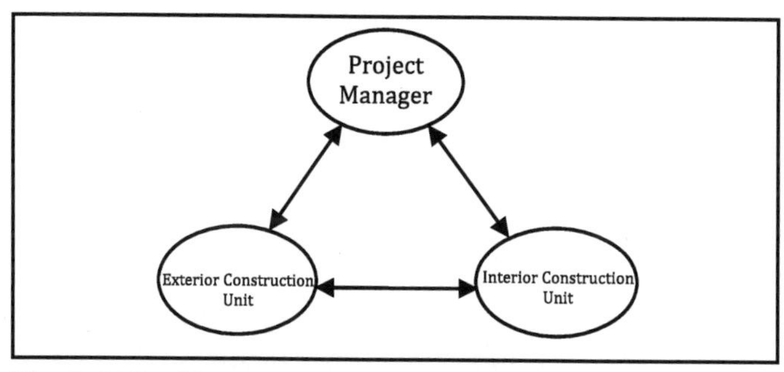

Fig 3.7 The "Growing Stage," Showing the Communication Between the PM and Two Units

If the project manager then appoints just one leader for each of the two units for the purpose of interactions, it simplifies the communication to just three people with six lines of communication open (back and forth arrow lines in three places gives six lines of communication). It is important that each line of communication is active. This stage of TEAM interaction is called the "Growing Stage" (Pasqualis, 2017).

This level of organization and involvement requires a propensity to excellence and skillful interaction and is therefore not open to mediocre thinkers and leaders. Such project communication plans with complex interactions must be designed to ensure proper flow of communication and address the 3Rs of communication in project management, i.e.

- Remove surprises
- Retain support
- Reassure the members of the TEAM

8. **The Conflict Management Function:** Mitigating friction and ensuring open lines of communication between TEAM members and across TEAMs are also vital aspects of communication. Effective conflict management helps to promote positive disagreements while limiting the negative effects of such conflicts. It may not be practicable to totally eliminate conflict, especially non-toxic forms; this is because the need for change, differences in perspectives, and different internal and external factors may lead to conflict situations. The focus must be to mitigate toxic conflict and encourage productive disagreements. The leader should constantly communicate a sense of solidarity, professionalism, and mutual respect but should not shout down divergent views even when they are passionately expressed. That conflict situation

might just be what the organization needs for a breakthrough idea, but a leader that doesn't have the communicative mastery to foster a sense of oneness and synergy after times of disagreements will allow a toxic environment to fester. In extreme cases, this could lead to high employee turnover, which could wreck the organization if it operates in a competitive environment where rivals are looking to poach good hands from other firms.

9. **The downward and upward interface function:** Downward communication should have five objectives (NIAEM, 2012), i.e., to instruct employees about their specific job roles and tasks; enlighten new employees about organizational processes, practices, and procedures; clarify the rationale for assigned tasks; provide the information and tools that various units and departments need to function, and provide evaluative assessments and feedback to subordinates on their performance. While the downward function is directive and hierarchical, outstanding leaders go a step further to encourage upward communication from their subordinates. This helps to foster an open-door policy, redresses grievances and complaints quickly (many adopt an ombudsperson approach), strengthens mentorship, and encourages participation in decision-making.

10. **The lateral and interactive interface function:** Mediocre leaders often have a problem with coordinating activities across departments, units, or chains of command. The lateral function of communication requires that leaders have a strong presence of mind, especially in an organization with multiple units and departments in which they oversee more than one or have to interact with others to get their tasks done. This is because leaders overseeing more than one unit need to be up and doing, while those interacting with colleagues in other units have to be proactive, interactive, and

synergistic in their approach. These communicators are called "boundary spanners," and their roles require that they accumulate and filter vast amounts of information across the organization. It is important that the facilitative roles they play should not be left to the microscopic leanings of average leaders.

The interactive function of communication happens within single units or groups in which group members need to interact effectively to ensure clarity, synergy, and high performance. Information sharing, task coordination, problem-solving, and conflict resolution all involve the interactive function of communication. Fostering upbeat interaction between group or TEAM members requires that the leader creates an atmosphere for such levels of interaction. Interactions are bound to happen, but the quality of such interactions is often dependent on the prevailing culture within the group or TEAM. Interactive communication can be of two kinds:

- **Networking:** This is an informal way of people who have common information and business interests within or without an organization making contact and exchanging information. When people are informally engaging in active information sharing internally or externally, they are said to be networking. Average leaders are not good at networking, and it explains why they are not up to date with happenings in the organization, in the market, or in the industry in which they operate.

- **Grapevine Interaction:** This is like a supplement to the formal channels of communication, and it usually carries impressions about the unspoken rules, assumptions, patterns, and happenings in an organization at an informal level of interaction between employees. When leaders do not show integrity, consistency, and professionalism, it reflects in the grapevine information that passes around. Assessing the situation of the grapevine in an organization can be a good way to tell the quality of leadership in place.

Understanding the Communication Process

Communication is essentially a two-way engagement, though it is possible to have one-way information dissemination; for communication, it must involve at least two people, i.e., a sender and a receiver. All communication involves transmission from a sender to a receiver and feedback from the receiver to the sender.

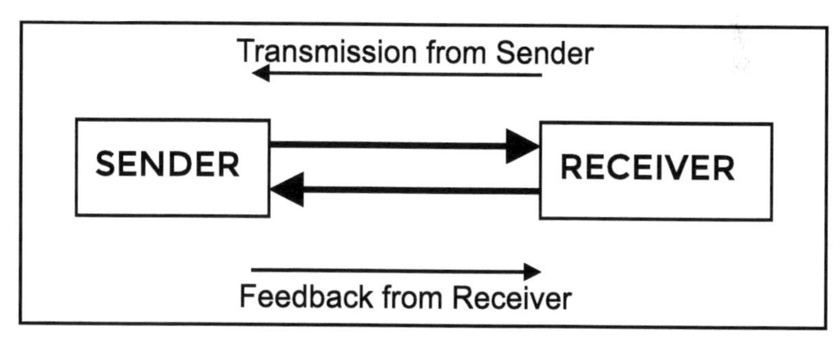

Fig 3.8 Two-way Communication between "Sender" and "Receiver"

Communication can be verbal, non-verbal (though physical), and written. It involves eight major steps:

a. *Identify the message that is to be transmitted.* At this point, the sender identifies what is to be transmitted and is clear about it.

b. *Encoding the message.* At this stage, the sender selects the most appropriate words, symbols, pictures, and the best medium for transmitting the information, message, or thought.

c. *Transmitting the message.* The sender or encoder then goes ahead to ensure the message is transmitted through whatever medium that is most suitable and ensures that the channel of communication is free of barriers and hindrances. The encoder's goal is to ensure the receiver gets the message.

d. *Receiving the message.* This is when the message reaches the receiver, or the receiver gets it. If the message is orally delivered, the receiver is to pay close attention to prevent information loss.

e. *Decoding the message.* After the message has been received, the receiver must process it to decode the meaning of the message. While it is the responsibility of the sender to get the message across and to make it as simple as possible, the receiver has to process the message to decode the meaning. Once the receiver understands the message, it is said that the sender has "gotten through" to the receiver.

f. *Acceptance or rejection of the message.* The receiver can then decide to either accept the message or reject it in part or in full after the message has been understood, depending on the possible implications of the message.

g. *Using the information.* The receiver may then use the information immediately, act on it, react to it, store it for future use, or discard it.

h. *Giving feedback.* The communication cycle or loop is only complete when the receiver gives feedback in the form of a response, acknowledgment of the message, or request for clarification. Communication can only be said to have taken place or to be taking place when the receiver sends feedback. The nature of the feedback is usually dependent on the context of the ensuing communication.

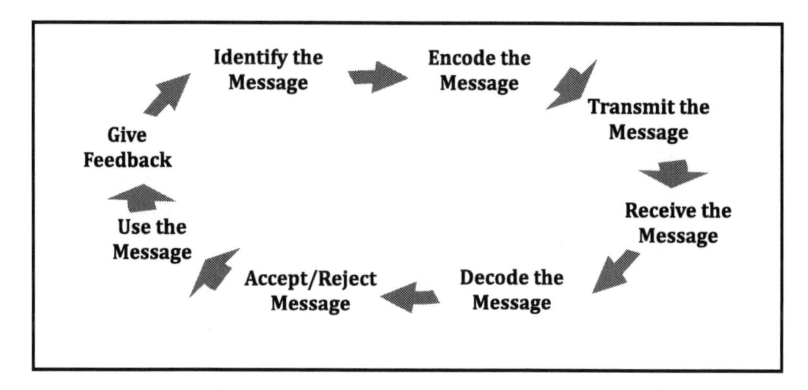

Fig 3.9 Communication Process Loop

CHAPTER FOUR

UNFOUNDED MORAL PRINCIPLES

"The moral values, ethical codes, and laws that guide our choices in normal times are, if anything, even more, important to help us navigate the confusing and disorienting time of a disaster."
—Sheri Fink

Case Study: 1MDB Fraud

Originally 1MDB (1Malaysia Development Berhad) was a Malaysian state fund established in 2009 by Najib Razak, the prime minister at that time, to promote development through foreign investment and partnerships.

In recent years, the fund has been at the heart of one of the biggest corruption scandals globally. The US justice department believes more than 4.5 billion US Dollars was stolen. The resulting scandal led to the toppling of a government and the arrest of Najib, his wife Rosmah Mansor, and a number of close associates.

Based on some leaked financial documents, 1MDB was a center of fraudulent activities from the outset. Massive sums were borrowed through government bonds and siphoned into bank accounts in Singapore, Switzerland, and the US. The huge sum of US$731m appeared in the personal bank account of Najib prior to the 2013 election. The money was said to have been used to pay off politicians, Najib's credit card bills and fund his wife's extravagant shopping habits. However, Najib denies the allegations, insisting that a Saudi prince donated the money.

Outside of the country, proceeds from the scandal were said to be used to fund the lavish lifestyle of one of the consultants in charge of overseeing 1MDB, Malaysian businessman Jho Low. Under Low's management, it was alleged that the fund bankrolled purchases including billions of dollars' worth of property in Beverly Hills and Manhattan. Some of the purchases included an apartment once owned by Jay Z and Beyoncé; a $260m yacht; a $35m private jet; a $3.2m Picasso gifted to Leonardo DiCaprio; a birthday party for Low where Busta Rhymes, Jamie Foxx, Chris Brown, Pharrell Williams, and Ludacris performed live, and Britney Spears jumped out of a cake; US$85m in Las Vegas gambling debts; and US$8m in diamonds for Australian model Miranda Kerr.

In addition, millions of dollars allegedly went towards funding the film, the Wolf of Wall Street, via a production company by Najib's stepson, Riza Aziz. However, Low maintains his innocence.

Until 2015, the alleged embezzlement of 1MDB money between 2009 and 2012 went unchallenged. It was in 2015 that British journalist Clare Rewcastle-Brown, who ran the website Sarawak Report, was handed 227,000 leaked documents detailing the depth of the fraud. The Wall Street Journal also managed to obtain the documents.

The Malaysian anti-corruption agency (MACC) started investigating. When it was about to issue a warrant for the prime minister's arrest, Najib took action. During the "week of the long knives," he fired the attorney general, Abdul Gani, who was leading the investigation, the deputy prime minister Muhyiddin Yassin (who was also a 1MDB critic), and four other ministers who had talked about the scandal. The MACC offices were raided, with four officials getting arrested.

In addition, Najib's government refused to cooperate with any of the investigations in Singapore, Switzerland, and the United States. In 2016, the Najib-appointed attorney general cleared him of all wrongdoing, saying the issue had "comprehensively been put to rest."

Many people weren't convinced of Najib's declaration of innocence. Mahathir Mohamad, a former PM who had helped Najib to power, continued to be outspoken on the scandal. With a strong conviction that he was the only person that can act and find a way through the problem, he announced he would run against Najib in the general election in 2018. His opposition party won and was elected for the first time in Malaysian history, and immediately 1MDB became the issue of the day. Najib faces 42 charges across five separate trials and could face years in prison. While he has denied any wrongdoing, he has been found guilty of criminal breach of trust, money laundering, and abuse of power.

The discussion of moral principles in leadership necessarily comes under the subject of ethics and its rational constructs and implications in human relations, perceptions, and organizational engagements. There seems to be an established understanding in the literature on corporate leadership—particularly as it concerns leadership ethics—that emphasizes the pivotal role of leaders in shaping the ethical and unethical behaviors of employees in their organizations, units, or departments. Apart from the natural and logical assumption of the benefits of ethically sound leadership, an avalanche of studies have linked healthy ethical leadership to positive outcomes such as increased organizational commitment by employees, enhanced job performance and task delivery, pro-social synergy and mutual assistance, a culture of speaking, and job satisfaction—which itself has the added merit of reducing employee turnover— among other benefits (Avey, Wernsing, & Palanski, 2012; Tu & Lu, 2013; Ng & Feldman, 2015; Moore, Mayer, Chiang, Crossley, Karleskey & Birtch, 2018).On the flip side, unethical leadership has been linked to employee deviance and a medium culture for prevalent unethical practices among subordinates (Mayer, Aquino, Greenbaum, & Kuenzi, 2012; Mayer, Kuenzi, Greenbaum, Bardes, & Salvador, 2009). Thus, ethical/unethical practices come with positive or negative implications depending on what side of the divide a leader functions in.

There have been scholarly exercises that have attempted to narrow down what moral principles can be universally applied to leaders and how to define morality in a way that is applicable to people across diverse sociocultural, political, and religious backgrounds. In this regard, there have been numerous useful inputs that have brought some measure of objectivity and focus to the subject; however, there are certain unique challenges that mediocre leaders pose to the morality question as it relates to leadership. One of such challenges is their propensity to moral disengagement and the employment of cognitive inversion. This involves using distended logic or seemingly excusable reasons to bypass moral standards in such a manner that relieves them of what should ordinarily be the internal self-distress that comes with breaking such moral codes. Their mediocre appreciation for ethically sound conduct and values creates a cognitive response pattern that easily panders to unfounded, erroneous, and sometimes spurious grounds to morally disengage. This happens in relation to decisions of strict moral import or decisions in complex situations that are morally sensitive.

Mediocre Leaders and Moral Disengagement

In analyzing the roles of leaders in negatively shaping the moral cognition of their employees, reference is made to Bandura's eight cognitive measures that individuals who employ moral disengagement use in plying their intents. These eight mechanisms include:

i. **Moral Justification:** For instance, where leadership places a premium on results and gives the impression that the end justifies the means, employees will gradually become desensitized to ethical boundaries so long as results are achieved. They will likely begin to make statements like, "...well, Mark, the end justifies the means, I got the contract, and the company is better for it. Now we get to play on the big stage, thanks to me."

ii. **Euphemistic Labeling:** This is a situation in which harmful practices are given a substitute name in order to color them differently and downplay the weight of contravening moral principles and ethics through such practices.

iii. **Advantageous Comparison:** This is making an otherwise unethical behavior or action look good by comparing it with a more frightful alternative or outrageous possibility. It is presented in a way that suggests that immoral conduct is a preferable option in the circumstance than having to put up with an impending catastrophe otherwise.

iv. **Diffusion of Responsibility:** Sometimes referred to as the bystander effect, it is a situation in which people don't take action because a large number of other people are present or involved,, especially because they believe someone else will take action. Sometimes action is also not taken because no one wants to be held responsible if something goes wrong. For instance, a scenario in which an individual says nothing about employees that engage in budget inflation and raw materials theft in one of the state branches of a megacorporation could be because many of the regular, middle and some top management staff are involved and "everyone" seems to know about it. For such a worker, speaking up may hold several risks, one of which is that the next person up the chain may be involved, and so the difficulty of knowing who to report to and the possibility that it could backfire becomes a restraint. Staying within the shadows of the large group provides anonymity that prevents him from being singled out. In other instances, it could be because you don't want to attract unnecessary attention or because you feel someone else might already be doing something about it. Some people take advantage of this atmosphere of diffused responsibility to perpetrate unethical acts.

v. **Displacement of Responsibility:** A good example of displacement of responsibility is a situation, for instance, in which an individual absolves himself of blame for any moral wrong by saying he was just acting on orders. In situations where leaders demand absolute obedience, this could become a cognitive thought pattern for subordinates to carry out grave atrocities even when they know the person giving the strange orders has no authority to do so.

vi. **Distortion of Consequences:** Distortion or disregard of consequences is a posture in which the consequences of certain unethical actions are deliberately ignored, minimized, downplayed, distorted, or even disbelieved. It is a cognitive and behavioral mode of moral disengagement that directly belittles, distorts, or trivializes the consequences of unethical conduct.

vii. **Dehumanization:** This happens when people are belittled of their "humanness" or when they are deliberately objectified and given a degrading name or status outside of their humanity in order to justify treating them with less dignity, empathy, understanding, or rectitude. For instance, classifying people into negative social groups can make them be treated discriminatorily as non-humans or sub-humans, thereby further leading to their dehumanization. It also gives the perpetrators of such acts a sense of moral justification because they have construed the circumstance differently. Leaders who view their workers as people who need to be driven hard to deliver the goods will likely engage in dehumanization.

viii. **Attribution of Blame:** This happens as a form of neurotic defense in which instead of accepting responsibility for actions taken, others are blamed for the consequences of those actions, especially when they prove to be negative.

Mediocre leaders first display these behaviors and cognitive patterns of reason as a way of deflecting from a straight moral course and sidelining the import or sensitivity of the unethical elements they have introduced in the decision-making process. These deviations are primarily activated when the boundaries of self-regulation within the leader are blurred by circumstantial pressures or environmental influences (from within and outside the organization). These pressures or influences test the sense of propriety, competence level, or long-term perspective of the leader, to which the deviating leader gives in, using any of the eight mechanisms mentioned above. Mediocre leaders exhibit an average cognitive ability to handle complexities and often find themselves making decisions from a borderline position that alternates between staying within safe, ethical boundaries and (slightly) bending the rules. This gradual desensitization potentially makes these leaders dangerous because, through repeated cycles of such practices, they subtly metamorphose into outright immoral leaders. Bandura (1999) puts it this way:

"Disengagement practices will not instantly transform considerate persons into cruel ones. Rather, the change is achieved by gradual disengagement of self-censure. People may not even recognize the changes they are undergoing. Initially, their self-reproof has been diminished through repeated enactments...until eventually... inhumane practices become thoughtlessly routinized [Sic]." (Bandura, 1999, p. 203)

This has a negative impact on the organizations or units they lead because studies show that leaders are crucial influences in the framing of their employees' environments and their sense-making cognition (Moore et al., 2018). Over time, employees tend to shift their ethical evaluations to align with those of their leaders, and this in turn influences to what extent subordinates could become habituated in the use of moral disengagement —especially when their leaders actively engage in such practices. Consequently, a culture of habituated unethical conduct becomes pervasive in the organization through the influence of unethical mediocre leaders. This interrelationship can be depicted in the following diagram.

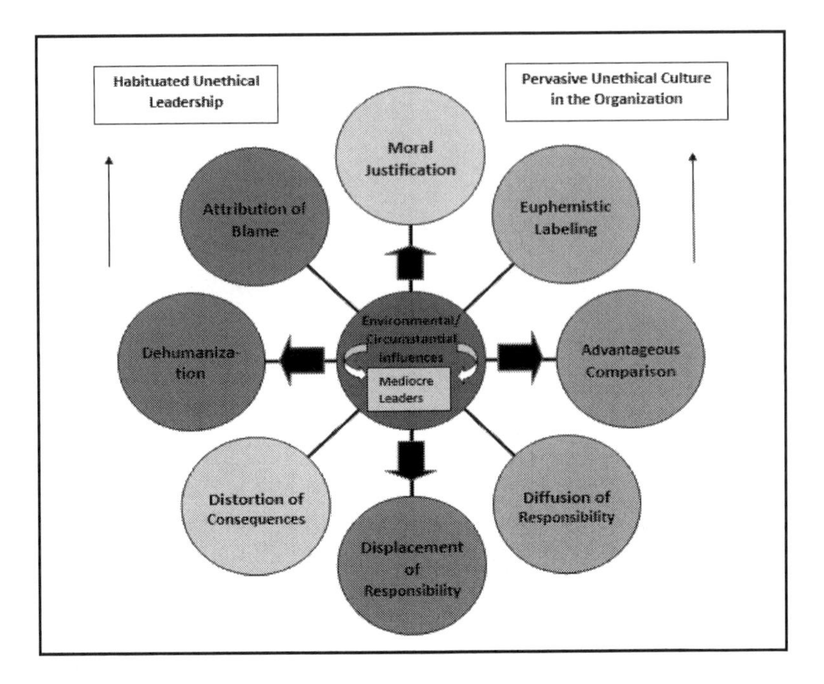

Fig 4.1 Interrelationship between Mediocre Leadership, Moral Disengagement, and Unethical Culture

Mediocre Leadership and the Propensity for Unethical Practices

Ethical leadership has been described as "the demonstration of normatively appropriate conduct through personal actions and interpersonal relationships, and the promotion of such conduct to followers through two-way communication, reinforcement, and decision-making" (Brown, Treviño, & Harrison, 2005, p. 120). This definition presupposes that for leadership to be ethical, it must demonstrate in its conduct at the personal, interpersonal and organizational levels such norms that are perceived as appropriate. It must also perpetuate such norms across the organization through two-way communication (transmission and feedback), reinforcement (rewarding the desired values and sanctioning the undesired ones), and inculcating these values in the decision-making process. Ethics are originally learned culturally, which is why a generalization of moral values must be based on some form of universal understanding of the moral principles being emphasized so that they are relevant across cultures. Furthermore, moral values are formed not only within the cultural context of society but also at the individual, group, and organizational levels through the processes of social enactment, social learning, and sense-making (Hannah, Lester, and Vogelgesang, 2005).

Identifying those values and norms that could be designated as universal in the 21st Century corporate life would therefore stem from internally adopted corporate codes of ethics, globally recognized ethical standards, national laws, and business or corporate ethics documented in relevant literature. Schwartz (2005) has listed six ethical values as forming the core of universal principles that guide corporate codes of ethics, they are:

(a) **Trustworthiness:** This could be said to refer to such qualities as integrity, honesty, credibility, quality, and consistency.

(b) **Respect:** This addresses the ideal of cordial regard and esteem for others. It also includes due consideration for their feelings, sensibilities, and rights as human beings.

(c) **Responsibility:** This has to do with having a sense of duty, taking management or control of something, and being accountable on account of it.

(d) **Fairness:** This virtue emphasizes reasonable, impartial, and just treatment to all. It is conduct that shows no favoritism, discrimination, or bias toward one person over another or toward one group over another.

(e) **Caring:** Thoughtful, considerate, and humane treatment towards others. It involves showing understanding and empathy.

(f) **Citizenship:** This refers to the state of being vested with the rights, privileges, and duties of a citizen in relation to a group. It includes obedience to and compliance with duties, obligations, functions, and codes of conduct as stipulated by law.

The manifestations of unethical practices by mediocre and subpar leadership are also associated along the lines of the six core areas identified above. They include:

(I) **Dishonesty and lack of integrity:** Ethical deficits occasioned by dishonesty and the absence of integrity create uncertainties and destroy trust within the organization. This also negatively affects the corporate image and public perception of the organization when such dishonesty reflects in their public engagements. Without trust, leaders lose the credibility to lead and have to resort to force and other extraneous methods to achieve compliance; and with the air of uncertainty always hovering around the organization, employee turnover and decline of customer confidence in the products and services being offered by the organization are likely consequences.

(II) **Manipulation and mistreatment of employees:** Unethical leadership also manifests itself in the mistreatment of subordinates, the violation of their rights, and the use of toxic language in hierarchical relations. It also exhibits itself in the form of employee misuse, manipulative tendencies, and partisan favoritism. Leaders who don't show respect for people's rights, feelings, and sensibilities are unethical.

(III) **Exhibition of bias:** Mediocre leaders often show deficiencies in judgment and have a weak appreciation for objectivity, equity, and new ideas. Leaders who do not show objectivity in their judgment but exhibit a sentimental and partisan-like approach to evaluating situations are bound to be biased and cannot give fair judgment on matters. They will also tend to discriminate or show favoritism in their treatment of subordinates and subvert the tenets of equity and equality. This immoral conduct also makes such leaders close their minds to new ideas, especially if it doesn't come from them or their microcosm of favorites. This creates an atmosphere of inequality, unfairness and could breed marginalization and injustice within the organization.

(IV) **Evasive and weak behavior:** Mediocre leaders can also be evasive, dodgy, and are quick to blame others instead of taking responsibility for their failures. They evade responsibilities they consider too technical, herculean, or complex and redirect the blame for their failures to their subordinates. This evasive behavior could also manifest in the form of being aloof in the interpersonal and interactive aspects of the organization's daily activities or being absent at important meetings. Such evasive attitudes compromise ethical values and do not conform to the sense of responsibility that leaders should have. Leaders who evade their responsibilities and apportion blame for their failures fall under the category of immoral and unethical leaders. Also, leaders that are too weak to do the right thing, evade the tough moral questions, and are indecisive on specific subject matters of moral import, are also unethical leaders.

(V) **Lack of empathy:** Unethical leaders don't care about others and cannot empathize with them. They are slave drivers, emotionally hard, and can be unreasonable in their demands. They are oblivious to the need for skillful management of human agency in driving organizational objectives, and this lack of skill and empathy makes them abusive leaders. Lack of empathy defies ethical principles and makes leaders who exhibit such traits mediocre because they will have a hard time retaining good hands and wouldn't be able to manage, mobilize or motivate employees to high performance.

(VI) **Illegal and corrupt practices:** Mediocre leaders who are unethical are also found to be complicit in corruption charges, sharp practices, and other illegal conducts. Their moral disengagement also seeps into the violation of extant provisions of legal codes, and in many instances, they engage in serious criminal offenses (Eisenberg and Brodbeck, 2014).

(VII) **Circumvention of the organization's policies and interests:** Bending the rules and policies of the organization to suit immediate conveniences is another trademark of unethical leaders. They like to cut corners and circumvent the interest of the organization for their myopic inclinations or self-interests. When leaders refuse to address policy breaches, they can also be said to be guilty of unethical behavior and acts capable of undermining the legitimate interests of the organization.

(VIII) **Conflict of interests and selfish ambition/interests:** Unethical leaders many times also find themselves in situations where there is a conflict of their personal interest with that of the organization and could choose to be silent about it. This silence could be a result of the concealed nature of the conflicting interest and the attractive benefits that could accrue. When such habits are reinforced, they soon become normalized, and they soon begin to scheme to put themselves more in such situations of conflicting interests. Conceited mediocre leaders also exhibit from time to time untamed ambitions and selfish pursuits to the detriment of the organization or even their subordinates.

Construing the Parameters of Unethical Conduct

The above norms form the major values and moral principles that leaders are expected to comply with, and they also provide a context for the evaluation and description of unethical conduct and leadership. They can be broadly delineated into two major areas that provide the scale for the ethical evaluation of actions, which are:

- Universal norms and moral principles
- Legal codes and extant corporate regulations

Defining Unethical Conduct

When leaders develop a penchant for shifting the goalposts in the middle of the game, causing employees to genuflect to arbitrary whims and straying indulgences that deviate from the known rules of engagement; or when they distort facts and downplay the consequential repercussions of ethical breaches, such acts are either categorized as illegal or immoral. It is against the backdrop of these two ethical branches that such derelictions are immediately construed—i.e., such conducts are either said to be immoral or illegal, depending on the specific acts or practices. In sum, unethical conduct could be those acts that breach stipulated laws and regulations (i.e., illegal acts) or those that breach moral principles (i.e., immoral acts). Brown and Mitchell (2010: p.588) have captured these two streams of unethical conduct in their definition of unethical leadership. They define unethical leadership as "...behaviors conducted and decisions made by organizational leaders that are illegal and/or violate moral standards, and those that impose processes and structures that promote unethical conduct by followers."

Interestingly, the above definition includes an element in the behavioral garb of unethical leaders that points to a crucial factor in understanding the different manifestations that unethical leadership could take. It says that unethical leaders, by their actions, impose processes and structures that promote unethical conduct among their followers. This points to the far-reaching extent that unethical leadership goes into affecting the organization. Many leaders pretend that they aren't complicit in the unethical culture in their organizations, when in fact, they indirectly, and in many cases directly but surreptitiously, support the unethical practices of their subordinates. Such denials often collapse easily under closer scrutiny. However, there are those who, for some reason, have enough airs or the boldface to cut corners. They breach rules, prioritize their selfish interests, and mistreat or violate the rights of their subordinates with effrontery. They arrogantly show favoritism towards select individuals or groups and push organizational boundaries to extremes in order to achieve their goals. They have a larger-than-life approach to situations and show a gusto for their moral disengagement. Unfortunately, their fall often leaves a loud thud in its wake, and in many instances, the ripple effects of their myopia affect innocent employees, families, and even national economies.

Systematic, Unintentional, and Repeated Conducts

There is also another group of leaders who unintentionally conduct themselves at some point or continuously in unethical practices. These unintentional acts could be largely done in ignorance but have the same effect on the organization. Though the more curious question is, do we also designate leaders who unintentionally breach ethical codes as unethical? Or is there some distinction that should apply to them? Lašáková and Remišová (2015) provide useful insights that help to further enhance our perspective on the subject. They define unethical leadership as a"...process of intentional or unintentional, passive or active, and recurrent influencing that harms others, be it individuals, organization and/or society as a whole." This definition agrees largely with that offered by Einarsen, Aasland, and Skogstad (2007:209), which states that in order for a leader's behavior to be defined as destructive, "the leader must perform the behavior systematically and repeatedly and violating the legitimate interest of the organization." The import of these definitions is that for a leader to be termed unethical, the ethical breaches must be repeated violations that are systematically, intentionally, or as in this case unintentionally carried out. A leader might commit a momentary and single unethical conduct, but this doesn't imply he is unethical; for him to be unethical, the conduct must become recurrent. Even where the unethical conduct is unintentional, so long as it is recurrent, the leader will be said to be unethical despite the clear absence of motive or intention.

However, from purely deontological and teleological views, where the actions of the leader do not stem from ethical motivation and are not carried out with enough care to ensure they do not harm others or the organization, even when they are momentary and isolated actions, they fail the deontological and teleological tests respectively and should thus be termed unethical. The harmful consequences of unethical conduct will make the leader unethical, especially where the consequences could have been foreseen had the leader been more aware, conscious, or diligent. Nonetheless, regardless of whether there is awareness or not, because of the consequences of the unethical conduct which brings harm to the organization or the community, the leadership takes on the unethical tag, and the determining factor here is the resulting harm caused by the unethical conduct.

Active and Passive Influence

Unethical leaders may exert their negative influence in ways that are either active or passive. When the leader directly deviates from established legal or moral principles and norms, this is an active way of promoting an unethical culture. Employees and subordinates will take cues from the sidelining of such legal and moral rules and replicate the same at crucial points of decision-making when moral or legal rules seem to stand in the way. On the other hand, unethical leadership is also understood from the passivity of the leader towards the unethical behavior and culture of subordinates in the workplace. When immoral activities are not censured, they are indirectly encouraged, and this reinforces unethical conduct as a permitted and appropriate culture in the organization. Besides, leaders also could make decisions in relation to rules, procedures, and work processes that negatively influence the perception of employees to ethical values, and which could undermine the value or relevance of ethical principles. Where leaders also do not emphasize what the clear values of the organization are and do not deliberately show any importance of ethical alignment, the order within such organizations becomes loose, undefined, and dangerously passive, giving room for more unethical practices. This compounds the problem of unethical leadership.

Absentee Leadership

Mediocre leaders also have another tendency to passivity through their frequent actual absence, or the vacuum they create through their weak interpersonal relationships, poor sense of mission, and lax oversight. They may not intentionally or actively promote unethical practices; however, the systematic, physical and psychological distance they keep creates voids and vacuums that can stall progressive clarity, ease, and discipline among employees. This affects procedural requirements and workflow linkages and thus creates scenarios in which parallel structures, methods, and ideas emerge, which distort established moral and codified templates in the organization. These parallels are the result of improvised initiatives at complex or critical junctures when leadership is inaccessible, unavailable, or unapproachable. This aloof and disjointed frame of operation means that without the leader even noticing any discrepancies or the resulting dip in the organizational culture; workers could go all out to achieve anything they need to achieve via any means possible, including through sharp or unethical practices, in so far as they deliver the results.

Lawful and Legitimate Interests

It is not in every situation that the originally stated objectives and internal rules of an organization are legitimate and lawful;

therefore, it is expected that leaders in acting in the best interest of the organization are also conscious of whether such interests are legitimate. The definition of what could amount to the legitimate interest of an organization has been explicated to mean "what is lawful, justifiable and in the best interest of an organization, the latter being defined by established internal rules and by internal formal power structures and procedures" (Einarsen, Aasland, Skogstad, 2007:210). Three things stand out here, the first is the legal compliance that such interests must align with, the second are actions that are justifiable (i.e., that enhance or align with moral principles in the organization), and the third is codified internal rules. Where the internal morals and rules of the organization contradict extant laws of the land, regardless of whether they claim to serve the interests of the company, such interests are unethical and illegitimate. Where they also contradict established rational moral principles of society, whatever other interests they claim to serve in relation to the organization are also at best illegitimate and unethical.

A case in point is where in order to serve the supposed best interests of an organization, the management unreasonably intrudes into the privacy of its employees; such "best interests" in view of such privacy breaches become questionable, illegitimate, and ultimately unethical. Organizational interests should be formulated in a way that respects the rights of others and clarifies the boundaries within which they can be expressed without infringing on the freedom and legitimate interests of others. Where such interests violate individual rights (whether within or without the organization), industry interests and rules, or the communal and societal values in which they operate, they can also be said to be illegitimate and unethical. Pless and Mark (2011) have further posited that where leaders through their actions or inactions undermine or harm other people, other organizations in their industry or outside their industries, and the community or society in which they operate, their leadership is said to be unethical.

It is important to conclude this chapter on the note that there are certain environmentally induced factors that make it possible for mediocre and unethical leaders to get involved in unethical practices, such as when there are no consequences for their poor delivery and unethical conduct, and when there is a poor accountability structure in place to enforce ethical values (Odole, 2018). Other reasons could include the prevalent culture in the social environment, unrealistic goals and targets set for employees that induce excessive pressure, and stringent conditions for remuneration, allowances, and bonus considerations. Also, where employees are attracted to the perks of an office or achievement, they tend to indulge in unethical practices in order to get to those positions or achieve those goals "on time."

CHAPTER FIVE

RESISTANT TO CHANGE

"Most suffering comes from the failure to adapt and a resistance to change."
—Debasish Mridha

Case Study: Kodak

Founded in the late 1880s, Kodak became a giant in the photography industry in the 1970s but filed for bankruptcy in 2012. For about a hundred years, Kodak was at the forefront of the photography industry with dozens of innovations and inventions, making photography accessible to the consumer. The company dominated the photographic film market during most of the 20th century. However, the company blew its chance to lead the digital photography revolution as they seemed to be in denial for too long.

Steve Sasson, the Kodak engineer, is said to have invented the first digital camera back in 1975. According to him, "But it was filmless photography, so management's reaction was, 'that's cute—but don't tell anyone about it." The management of Kodak did not see digital photography as a disruptive technology. According to a former vice-president of Kodak, Don Strickland, "We developed the world's first consumer digital camera, but we could not get approval to launch or sell it because of fear of the effects on the film market." They were so focused on the film's success that they missed the digital revolution after being the first to discover it.

The Kodak failure startled many. In the 1980s, the photography industry started shifting towards and embracing the digital. With Kodak inventing the digital camera, it would have been logical for them to enter into the digital space; however, the company jumped on the digital trend bandwagon as a late adopter while still selling analog cameras and film. As a matter of fact, rather than focus on making relevant changes to adapt to the digital movement, Kodak developed a new business direction—printers. They focused on the printing industry, making expensive printers and inexpensive ink.

Interestingly, digital cameras were not the only revolutionary products back then. Smartphones were already becoming ubiquitous, and digital camera producers saw their sales dropping. People were moving from printing pictures to storing them on digital devices or sharing them online on social media platforms.

Prior to Facebook, Kodak made a business move to purchase a photo-sharing site called Ofoto in 2001. However, instead of doing what Instagram later did, Kodak used Ofoto to get more people to print digital images—it missed the point of the digital movement. This was a wrong move. In 2012, while Kodak was filing for bankruptcy, Facebook acquired Instagram, the new bubbling photo-sharing social network, for $1 billion.

There are specific lessons to learn from the failure of Kodak. It is fascinating that many companies tend to see the disruptive forces affecting their industry, and they often invest considerable funds to engage in emerging markets; their failure, however, is usually an inability to fully embrace the new business models inspired by the disruptive change. Kodak produced a digital camera, invested in the technology, and even understood that photos could be shared online; nevertheless, they failed to catch the message—online photo sharing was actually the new business, it was not another way of extending the printing industry.

Kodak's lack of strategic creativity and inability to see business and market challenges from a different perspective made it misinterpret the same line of work and industry that it was operating in, which became significantly impacted by a fundamental shift towards the digital age. Strategic problems may demand more than a single set of approaches to problem-solving, but if we remain rigid, we can miss significant moments to make the shift. Kodak did not realize this as its leadership seemed frigid about change and risks; instead, they developed procedures and policies to sustain the status quo and their old business models, which eventually led to failure.

Isn't it amazing that the name IBM still stands tall, relevant, and full of life today, even after a hundred and seven years of existence? This next-to-miraculous organization has kept many people wondering how a company that started in 1913 still remains a successful industry leader despite the cut-throat dynamics of the tech world. But a closer look at its ingenious commitment to innovation, change, and sensitivity to market dynamics makes it stand out as a primus inter pares. It is clear from IBM's success story that its leadership model is effective, robust, dynamic, forward-looking, and adaptive. IBM started as a company selling mechanical tabulating machines, but today the $100 billion company makes most of its revenue from selling software and other on-demand services that didn't exist fifty years ago. It didn't stay rigid! So, the real questions you should be asking are: "Are you rigid?" Are your leaders rigid? Do your employees prefer the old way of doing things? Or are they proactive and observant of changing times and trends? Mediocre leaders are rigid, are fixated on traditional ways, and are usually resistant to change.

Rigid Leaders

Leadership strategy analyst Dina Gerdeman, in an interview article for the Harvard Business School Working Knowledge (HBS Working Knowledge), evaluated opinions expressed by other experts on why companies that were once great, giant brands, and "world-beaters" failed. The article noted that they all went down for essentially the same reason, which is that the leaders of those great names and brands were rigid in one way or another. They suffered from a failure of leadership to successfully understand changing times because their leaders were either unable or unwilling to sense new opportunities. Therefore, these leaders couldn't reconfigure their organizations' resources and assets in ways that could help them seize new opportunities, stay relevant in the market, and open new streams of prosperity. In order words, they became overtaken by the fast pace of the changing realities and lost out in the market. There are important skills and tools that can help leaders remain innovative and productive; however, rigidity—which is one of the major tragedies of mediocre leadership—is a proven way to kill continuity, growth, and the potentials for new streams of success.

Experts have noted that business leaders can dodge failure if they adopt an "ambidextrous" approach in carrying out their business activities (Tushman and O'Reilly III, 2016). This means that if they continue investing in quality and in the excellent delivery of their current products and services while ensuring at the same time to strive for growth and innovation in new areas, they will find opportunities to innovate or to offer new products and services. Companies can become long-term successes if they have leaders with flexibility and good innovative drive and leaders who are deliberate about scouting for viable business prospects and making internal changes to prepare their organizations for the future. Rigidity in an organization could manifest itself in the form of over-centralization, too much compartmentalization, an overly hierarchical structure, and the difficulty or restriction of staff from functioning in different roles (Iyanda, 2020). Among other possible factors, there are two clear elements that shape the culture of rigidity in a leader; they are ego-related problems or excesses and inertia (Iyanda, 2020).

When leaders have an exaggerated image of themselves, or on the flip side, if they begin to negatively question and second-guess themselves, they tend to become rigid and inert (Campbell, 2014). In terms of inertia, apart from the fact that rigid leaders don't take relevant action to engage innovative processes and fresh ideas, inertia also reflects in their organizational management style through resource rigidity—i.e., failure to enhance resource investment patterns and routine rigidity—i.e., failure to enhance internal processes (Iyanda, 2020). In this way, they fail to internally invest their resources and restructure their internal processes in vital areas that can keep them competitive. They are instead prone to act late, if at all, and even at that, with a fire brigade approach. As the popular saying goes, "change is the only constant thing in life," and we are increasingly swamped with happenings that make this wise nugget invaluable. Today's socio-economic, political, and technological environments lend credence to the ever-changing dynamics in which we live, and they reinforce this vital lesson that all great leaders are conscious of, which is that they must be deliberate about seeking progressive changes and taking relevant actions to engender these progressive changes in the interest of their organizations.

Why Mediocre Leaders are Resistant to Change

Mediocrity, as has been noted in previous chapters, is a fault that makes leaders confined to their own microscopic perspective and too preoccupied with their own thoughts, self-image, and insecurities. However, it is amazing how driven leaders can initially be on their journey up the ladder and willing to go to great lengths, learn new things, entertain new ideas and employ new methods to prove themselves. However, once they reach the top many just seem to plateau and stop growing. Such leaders were originally motivated by naked ambition and had neither learned the vital people skills nor developed strategic and critical thinking abilities needed while on their way up. They soon become problematic because they lack the required foresight and may be too insecure—and sometimes too opinionated—to learn.

This brings to mind the story of a famous former CEO in a tech firm whose contract wasn't renewed due to certain emerging sales difficulties after many years of providing strategic leadership and creating great changes and successes in the firm. He was, however, employed by another leading firm within the same tech industry—though in a slightly different environment

—but got fired in less than a year after the company incurred great losses and made some fundamentally flawed strategic decisions that almost sank the entire value of the company. It is sometimes difficult to accurately analyze these things and what may have gone wrong; nonetheless, from interviews granted by the said CEO and by other sales partners who worked closely with him at the first tech firm, the picture began to look more like a leader who had reached a plateau and suddenly wasn't able to successfully interact with the new thinking, new developments and new challenges within the industry. While no leader can be said to be above mistakes, leaders have a responsibility to objectively evaluate their performance on a regular basis and see what they might be missing, especially when subordinates, stakeholders, and rapidly changing events around them may be pointing to outdated methods or other missing links. This brings us to the first reason why mediocre leaders are vulnerable to change.

The Syndrome of Success-induced Complacency

It is possible for leaders who have made grievous mistakes in the past to learn from their mistakes and recover from their damaged reputation, just as there are indicators of a reputation recovery for the former chief executive referred to in the scenario cited above. Nevertheless, organizations must focus with delicate attention on leaders whose decisions have serious implications on their corporate performance, the investment portfolios of their shareholders, and the jobs and long-term careers of their employees. As we have learned from the global economic meltdown that occurred in 2008, leaders who are at the peak of their careers, who sit at the top of economically strategic organizations, and who oversee sensitive assets need systems of checks and accountability because, at such heights, they are vulnerable to the complacency of the success syndrome. They are susceptible to factors such as burnout, disorientation, excessive ambition, and overconfidence. Others include unethical conduct, being laid back, inability to engage new ideas or challenges, regimented thinking, and old guard symptoms. This is why apart from offering fat bonuses and perks and the obsession with corporate governance—both of which are actually good considerations, every forward-looking organization should pay close attention to the corporate performance of their CEOs/top executives on a regular short-term evaluative basis. This will help them identify potential problems early enough so that they can make adjustments before major problems arise.

The point being made here on why leaders are resistant to change is that where a person's needs and desires are already met, and where leaders, especially those in the corporate world, have achieved great feats and comfort for themselves, there is a greater temptation to become complacent and self-absorbed. This is why there is a need for greater emphasis on accountability and performance for corporate leaders as a determinant of their continued relevance. This will help curtail any excessive sense of entitlement that may tend to weaken the urgency of responsibility and sense of duty that leaders should have due to the high stakes involved in their assignments. When leaders know that they are accountable for performance regularly, despite how valued they are by the organization, they will be more circumspect. This will also help the organization to know when a leader is no longer in the best build, state of mind, or ethical frame. This will help it take the necessary restorative, corrective, or definitive steps in the interest of the organization. Steve Tobak (2012) puts it aptly when he says, "...while a merit-based structure that depends on the relationship between accountability and success may not be perfect, it's way better than the alternative—an entitlement-based structure where there's no personal responsibility whatsoever."

1. Inability to Adapt to New Ways

One of the stark realities of leadership in the 21st Century is that leaders who do not want to become outdated and grow out of relevance must be adaptable. They must be willing to constantly engage the trilogy of learning, unlearning, and relearning in relation to the new ideas, knowledge, innovative developments, and emerging trends in the immediate and expanded environments in which they transact business. The view of Schein (2015) is apposite in identifying five related elements that will make leadership in the 21st Century increasingly complex. These five elements are captured in the diagram below.

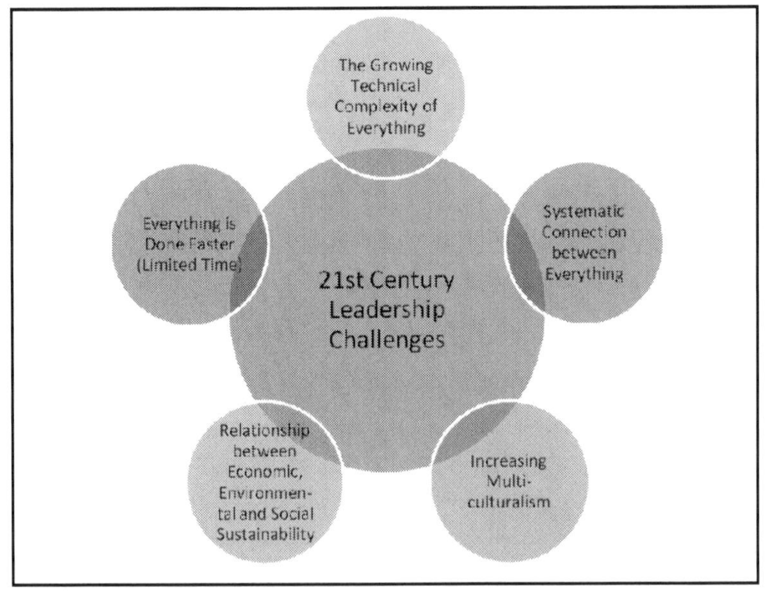

Fig 5.1 E.H. Schein's Five Elements that Increase Contemporary Leadership Complexity (2015)

Adaptability is best interpreted as a leader's willingness to do things differently in order to keep the organization responsive, innovative, and relevant to the changing dynamics in the business environment. This is in the interest of the organization's sustainability and to increase the opportunities for maintaining and multiplying its success. Although it is important to take into cognizance that there is a growing technical complexity that organizations have to face today as they engage with their environments. This is evident in the compulsive escalation of innovation and technology that is constantly redefining the space in which they do business. In addition to this fact, everything seems connected these days. One event in a seemingly remote human activity/geography now has a systemic connection with almost every other thing. This means that ripple effects both in the negative and positive senses can spread from one end to the other because of the growing systemic connection in our world.

The foregoing analysis is also apt in explaining the context of sustainability in connection with the increasing interrelationship between our economic activities, the protection of our physical environment, and the importance of social responsibility and cohesion. The depletion of the physical environment through our economic activities poses a grave danger to our economic future and physical existence, while an upsurge in social instability and irresponsibility will lead to social stress and adversely impact the business environment. The increasing rate of global workforce diversity as a result of globalization and technological development also has complex implications for markets, jobs, and economic production, with all of these changes taking place in a fast-paced manner, leaving no room for sluggishness.

As Bonita Richter (2018) puts it, "A business challenge that is becoming more acute is that the rate of change is accelerating." There is a time factor to the decision-making process, which is why maximizing information channels is critical to leadership because it accelerates decision-making while also ensuring a rich diversity of inputs that could lead to sound decisions. There is a tendency for mediocre leaders to think that widening the consultation net slows down the decision-making process; however, not all decisions can be taken having not gathered vital data. Handy and valuable data is easier to source when we involve the right people, and this helps to better facilitate decision-making. So, it is important to value information channels and ensure a quick translation of the information into tangible decisions that can benefit the firm.

Until leaders are willing to do things differently and engage others, they will remain rigid and become potential liabilities to the organizations they lead. So, while everything seems dependent on leadership, leaders need to learn early that they will be more dependent on the network of human resources that they can directly or indirectly benefit from. Leaders who refuse to gain valuable perspectives from market trends, their subordinates, customers, shareholders, industry experts and analysts, colleagues, active agents in the value chains, and even their friends and family are rigid. This rigidity will cut them off from relevant information and crucial perspectives on new trends. They will also have to keep using or recycling outdated information and methods because they are cut-off from the new. Mediocre leaders who aren't flexible and bendable in the eye of today's stormy environment will break the ship and sink everyone. To be adaptable, leaders will have to:

- Cast off arrogance and put on humility as they need support from others to succeed.
- Move from talking too much to listening more. Today's leaders will always need to know more; therefore, their information drive must be stronger.
- Encourage the free flow of information upward and vertically. They will need to create a favorable atmosphere that enables their subordinates, colleagues, stakeholders, experts, and those in their close social circle to share the knowledge and information they have.

2. They are Bound by a Stack of Personal Barriers

When leaders show intolerance for change or new ideas, it could also be because they are trying to hide their inadequacies. Whether it is fear/the absence of courage, inadequate knowledge, skill deficiency, lack of clarity, inadequate planning, or they are absorbed by a sense of insecurity—there are various personal barriers that could be holding them back. Let's take a closer look at some of these personal barriers.

(a) **Fear and lack of courage:** Fear is not a new emotion, and psychologists tell us it is a natural human emotion —i.e., we all at some point have our fears. The problem is when we allow fear to take hold of us until it immobilizes us, it becomes toxic. We can address our fears by projecting the worst-case scenarios of our decisions against the best that could happen. We could then highlight practical steps that could help mitigate the chances of failure and increase the chances of success, after which we set what we consider as our acceptable threshold for going ahead with the decision. If we put our threshold at 80%, for instance, it would mean that if we can establish an 80% chance of success, we are ready to go ahead with the decision.

It is also important to assess the risks and properly interpret what their impact could be on the organization. Where the 20% risk of failure is capable of inflicting consequences of enormous proportions, we can step down the decision and try out other ideas. The important thing is not to be frozen by fear and to be courageous about expanding the opportunities of the organization. Where we have a favorable chance of success, the next thing is to act on it—this is what courage is about. Delaying action is a possible sign that our sense of fear is stronger than our desire to succeed despite the fair chances for success. Leaders will always have to deal with uncertainties and risks, but what they do with uncertainty and how they manage the attendant risks is what distinguishes courageous leaders from indecisive and mediocre leaders. Even the snail changes its shell – a sign that it is alive and growing.

(b) **Ignorance:** The cure for ignorance is knowledge. Leaders must identify what they need to know to be successful in their new roles and occupy themselves with consuming information and acquiring knowledge in those areas. Remaining frigid, withdrawn, and closed to change because it is in an area in which the leader has limited knowledge is the mediocre thing to do. Instead, leaders should be open to learning from those who are well-knowledgeable in the subject matter, even if they are subordinates. Leaders should be open to taking relevant courses, buying relevant materials, attending seminars and workshops, and building contacts with people within and outside the organization who can be of help.

(c) **Poor skills:** Like ignorance, incompetence also dampens the confidence of a leader. A leader who does have the relevant soft skills and technical abilities needed to deliver on the job will be reluctant to lead any initiative or drive for the organization. And like ignorance, the cure for this is to acquire the relevant skills. Leaders need to constantly engage themselves in training and mentorship arrangements that could help them develop their leadership skills and improve their professional competence.

(d) **No plan:** Mediocre leaders are defective in the area of planning. This is one reason they may be unwilling to lead change or may want to resist it. They consider planning quite herculean, and they are too laid back to get involved in the process. Such leaders do not deserve to lead because leadership requires a great deal of stock-taking, a great deal of brainstorming, and a great deal of networking in order to execute a project. It is during planning that leaders can develop a method, which becomes a handy resource for the effective execution of their leadership goals and objectives. This brings us to the next point.

(e) **Indifference and lack of clarity:** This is a situation in which a leader hasn't clearly identified a vision and purpose and has not clearly spelled out the goals and objectives that he wishes to pursue in line with the overall vision and objectives of the organization. When leaders do not have a visionary inclination, they cannot be visionary in their approach. It is the pursuit of a clear vision that propels action and brings energy to the TEAM. Indifference is a situation in which leaders aren't proactive about tackling specific issues and interests of customers, shareholders, employees, and internal processes. It includes not having a definitive mind and objective that addresses critical blocks of the organization. This flows primarily from not having a clear vision and well-defined objectives. As Hugh Blane (2017) puts it, "Indifference comes from not having a clear and compelling leadership purpose."

(f) **Inertia and a lack of positive energy:** Inertia sets in when we get lulled into the mundane routine of doing work in a simplistic way. While it is important to emphasize consistency in approach and style, it is more important to know when a style no longer works and to adapt to a more relevant approach. Mediocre leaders are asleep and want to remain in bed! They hate to get up and be alive to the day! When we approach our work each day with positive desires and connect our work to a bigger picture and a higher purpose, we are more energetic about it. We are more prone to keep up with trends in the industry, engage in research, try out initiatives that are connected with our jobs, and undertake projects that expand the scope of our understanding and its application. This makes us more practically involved and keeps us fresh with perspectives and ideas. Staying within the conservative zone of what is safe and predictable is a good prescription for going out of relevance quickly.

(g) **Poor Self-Image:** Leaders need to possess healthy self-esteem to be able to function at a high level. This esteem is also a source of morale boost and stability for the members of their TEAM that look up to them for guidance. When employees sense poor self-esteem in their leader, it dampens their expectations, makes them worried about their productivity, and dilutes their energy. It could lead to cynicism, pent-up frustration, and discouragement when they see that they have a weak leader who needs to "grow up." Positive self-affirmation is one way that a leader who struggles with poor self-esteem can apply in boosting their confidence. It is also important that they identify those factors that make them feel inadequate and evaluate the veracity of those preconceived notions. If they find any credibility in them, then what they need is to take action to resolve them. Getting professional help is also a great idea.

(h) **Misalignment of Organizational and Personal Incentives:** When leaders have a close-up opportunity to climb up the ladder, and they sense that acceding to or implementing certain changes may work against them, despite the benefits that might accrue to the organization from these changes, they will likely be reluctant. "Misalignment of personal incentives can cause us not to act; even when we know, it's the best thing for the company..." (Bosso, 2020).

Apart from these eight personal barriers just mentioned, there are other forms of barriers that could make mediocre leaders resistant to change and keep them stuck in their old track.

3. Organizational Barriers

Organizational barriers are those series of factors that occur within the organizational context that influence the leader's perception and response to change. Some of these barriers include:

(a) **Unavailable or limited resources:** One of the major reasons some leaders avoid undertaking projects or planning for them is that they know there are no resources to implement the changes. The financial, material and even human resources needed to carry out their transformational ideas do not seem available. There are instances where these shackles are real, but in many other instances, the leaders need to be more ingenious about solving their problems. Where the leader in question has significant influence over the decision to hire and fire, he has enough leverage there to bring about the needed human resources; but in the event that they are stuck with their staff, what they need is to engage the painstaking process of training.

It is a great idea working out a schedule and plan that is presented to top management with cogent reasons on why they need to implement the changes and how it will benefit the organization. The leader's persuasive appeal is vital here. However, where it is a matter of material and financial resources, it is important to make a solid connection to the financial value that those changes will bring to the organization and think of proactive ways to attract the funding they need through equity or debt. Leveraging other people's resources and outsourcing could also be some of the effective ways they could employ. One of the responsibilities of leadership is to solve problems, and where leaders engage their minds and those of their TEAM, they could hatch a short or long-term plan that will help them achieve their goals. What matters is that they are innovating for growth.

(b) **Mismanaging organizational priorities:** It is important to attend to urgent situations, but leaders need to avoid situations in which urgencies keep coming up because of their poor planning and unpreparedness. When leaders have to spend productive time attending to emergencies and putting out fires, they soon find themselves spending less time in actual strategic thinking and planning, and they become distracted, disorganized, and eventually, their organization begins to lag. Leaders should identify what is important for their organizations and ensure important things (like planning, market prospecting, etc.) get done at the right time while also ensuring that emergencies that arise are attended to.

(c) **Shareholder/stakeholder demands:** Leaders who don't interact sufficiently with their stakeholders to gauge their risk appetite and understand their core interests in terms of business prospects may be less willing to undertake projects or ventures that are not as certain as the traditional streams of revenue they are used to. The pressure to please stakeholders and not reduce the earnings of the company may inform the risk-averse nature of certain leaders. This makes them careful about changes and more conservative in their approach to spending. Nevertheless, leaders must realize that they need to scout for solid opportunities that will secure their place in the market, especially when market changes and dynamics may potentially reduce their current earnings. If they need to discuss with investors, then they should engage that option and ensure to secure a solid footing in whatever endeavor they seek and work to mitigate risks as much as possible.

(d) **Customer response:** This aspect of reluctance may have its benefits; as much as leaders need to be innovative and engage in change, they also need to ensure that the products and services they offer to the market are well received. Testing market response is important, and where customers show resistance to a change in product or service, there is a need to prevent loss through the cost of investing in such projects. Some executives have had their fingers burned with products they introduced into the market but which didn't get the right response. To prevent such, it is important to take customer feedback from surveys and controlled studies in the early stages of the product planning process. Product and service innovation should also be an ongoing activity rather than a sudden once-a-while action.

(e) **All is Well:** Why make changes when everything is going on just fine? Why can't we enjoy our success in peace and not rock the boat? The problem with this thinking is that it gets leaders to be laid back. This could get their organizations to also develop a laid-back culture, make them be overtaken by events and possibly threatened in the market. It is foolish to make radical changes that can cause confusion and tamper with the current success an organization may be enjoying; however, it is also unwise to keep your eyes closed to emerging trends and new opportunities to build on your success. In the world of business, you really can't be static; you are either on your guard and making progress; otherwise, you are surely moving backward because others are getting ahead of you—and they are sure to change things in the industry pretty fast. Staying innovative and relevant to the needs of your market is one of the most strategic activities that a business leader must constantly engage in.

CHAPTER SIX

INCONSISTENT MANAGERIAL PRACTICES

"When we overlook the errors of people we like and favor, we are crippling the society because others look up to them and are copying from them. They will also copy their errors. One day we will be complaining why things are like this."
—De philosopher DJ Kyos

Case Study: The One Where Rachel Smokes

"The One Where Rachel Smokes" is the 18th episode of the 15th season of "Friends" and the 115th episode in the overall series. This episode was first aired on NBC in the United States on April 8, 1999. In this episode, Rachel (Jennifer Aniston) begins a new job at Ralph Lauren, but she soon feels left out because she doesn't smoke, yet the real decision-making often takes place during smoking breaks. This makes her feel left behind. Rachel attempts to solve this problem by taking up the habit of smoking too, but she seems to find it challenging.

On her first day working at Ralph Lauren, Rachel attempts to get along with her new colleague and also with her boss, Nancy, and Kim, respectively. Both of them are smokers and usually go on cigarette breaks. Rachel couldn't join, and she is soon angered when she discovers that Nancy and Kim are busy making company decisions without her during the smoking breaks. This further makes Rachel fear for her position, as Kim and Nancy spend more time together smoking and bonding. She believes that if this continues, Nancy is probably going to get promotions while she would be left behind.

Therefore, to make an effort to bond with her co-workers, Rachel goes with them and joins them in smoking cigarettes. She is not enthusiastic at all to fall into the bad habit and even tries unsuccessfully to talk Kim and Nancy into quitting, as they end up smoking behind her back. It gets to the point that Kim warns Rachel that she (Kim) would fire her if she catches her with a cigarette, claiming that she did not want to "drag her down with them." Soon enough, viewers are able to see a correlation between the smoking breaks and Kim's growing fondness for Nancy. There is little, or no thought exercised when Kim shows her preference for Nancy as the co-worker that should go with her on a business trip to Paris. It is not clear what Kim's criteria were for choosing her partner for the trip, but her threat of firing Rachel as a response to Rachel's obsession "to belong" and "to be part of the decision-making process" says a lot about the clear signs of favoritism on Kim's part.

This episode relates graphically an important lesson about how employees who feel treated less than others can sometimes grovel for attention and want to be part of the inner circle with their colleagues. They feel that their career growth, privileges, and security in the workplace are threatened when they are left out of the loop, while a select few who are on the same level as them in the organization enjoy more attention. Interestingly, Jennifer Aniston, who acted the role of Rachel, was actually a frequent smoker at the time of filming, but the important point is that beyond the artistic brilliance of the script and its production, the unique response and feedback that this episode got from the viewing public might be a testament to how people resonated with the events of the story in relation to their own work experience. The pressures felt by the least favorite employees are exemplified by Rachel's crave for more attention and inclusion.

In its original airing, "The One Where Rachel Smokes" was third in ratings for the week of April 5–11, 1999, having a Nielsen rating of 14.8, equivalent to about 14.4 million viewing households. The episode was the third highest-rated show on NBC that week, after ER and Frasier. With 1.76 million viewers, it was the most-watched program on the network the week it was released.

Whether you are a salesperson, janitor, waiter, administrator, executive, teacher, or parent, showing inconsistency in your behavior and preferences will undermine trust, cause confusion, increase individual and social stress in your group, and reduce the level of productive engagement of other members of the TEAM who have to collaborate with you in order to function. Mediocre leaders display inconsistency in different ways, such as preferential or differential treatment, incongruent decisions, disparate reactions to similar situations, and erratic application of organizational rules and personal principles. Inconsistency in your words and actions means that you are observed to be a different person when in a different setting, with different people, or at different times. Such inconsistency as a leader tends to make your subordinates and TEAM members insecure and apprehensive about what to expect from day to day because of the disturbing air of behavioral unpredictability that occasions your leadership. As a matter of fact, research shows that employees prefer identifying with consistent unfair treatment as the negative part of a leader's make-up, rather than the experience of a leader's inconsistent hopping between fairness and unfairness.

Leaders who entertain inconsistency in one area are susceptible to being inconsistent in other areas and are also exposed to the risk of brewing employee discontent and losing their credibility because of this weakness in their character (Jones, 2011; Whetten & Cameron, 2016, p. 441; Nguyen, 2019). This is not to say leaders are to be static, unbending, and dogmatic. Leaders need to apply different judgments to situations based on their immediate interpretation of things—i.e., there is no "one cap fits all" approach to resolving problems. Hence, responses could depend on the peculiarity of the circumstances; even when there might be some basic underlying similarities of the present case to previous situations, many times, there are still peculiarities. An old survey conducted by Skinner and Sasser (1977), which still applies today, provides a paradoxical account of how high-achieving managers have differed from those with mediocre performance.

The survey revealed that the highly accomplished managers showed typically "inconsistent" dexterity in how they handled situations. For instance, they knew what situations required them to get into the fine details and those in which they were to maintain a more strategic posture and avoid getting sidetracked with the details. They could delegate a lot at one time and delegate so little at another or could communicate verbally with some staff and more in writing with others, among other such similar interchanges of opposite responses. This kind of "inconsistency" seems to stem more from an intelligent interpretation of the situation and knowing what line of action is most appropriate at the material time. In such situations, subordinates and employees can tell that there is an organic consistency in the core values but that the leader thinks outside the box when necessary and is therefore dynamic in his response to situations. His decisions are based on the implications of what any adopted approach, decision, or response could have on the organization's objectives at the material time.

However, this is different from some whimsical deviation and inconsistency in the bottom-line character, credibility, objectivity, and fairness of the leader; it is a recognition of what can sometimes be the dialectical connection between consistency and inconsistency. Here consistency and inconsistency are understood as social constructions that emerge in relation to each other and in response to emerging environmental conditions (Edwards, 2017). For instance, in order to achieve certain organizational objectives, consistency in the use of an adopted public communication model may be emphasized. However, subsequent environmental complexities may require the introduction of certain "inconsistencies" in the communication model as an ongoing adaptive response to environmental changes. In the end, the goal is to ensure that the original objectives of the organization are not compromised, but consistency and inconsistency are constructively engaged as mutually beneficial opposites in achieving the same set of objectives. What is clear in all of these, however, is that the core values of the leader should discernibly remain congruent and that the management approach should essentially be consistent with the universal core values identified in Chapter Four. What may differ is the adaptive response of the leader in given environmental or situational conditions based on intelligent assessments and judgment. For instance, that a leader communicates more with a unit in writing may be due to the technical sensitivity of that unit and the need for specificity, as against the necessarily boisterous nature of another. What matters is that there is a clear sense of obligation to maintaining a balance in the perceptions of employees in both units and that the leader makes it clear in words and action that all units are strategic to the organization. This could, for instance, be achieved in the illustration just cited by ensuring that there are also opportunities for verbal interactions with the technical unit.

The erratic managerial tendencies of mediocre leaders will likely constitute a clog in the wheel of strategic decision-making. The critical importance of strategic decisions to the pulse of modern organizations requires that there is some measure of consistency in decisions of strategic inputs and outcomes. Erratic strategic decisions can be described as inconsistent managerial judgments that determine the direction of the firm. Reviews of findings show that erratic decisions are often associated with less optimal results (Mitchell, Shepherd, & Sharfman, 2011). Erratic or inconsistent judgments tend to pose higher diminishing impacts on the quality of decisions made, and this is because the decision-maker doesn't follow a clear-cut decision model in the decision-making process. According to Karelaia and Hogarth (2008), a good decision-making model that will eliminate inconsistent/erratic decision-making should incorporate three things:

- *A Matching Index*—i.e., important factors/components that form the critical cues in the leader's particular environment and which should inform the major considerations in the decision-making exercise.

- *Environmental Predictability*—i.e., what are the likely variations, differences, and peculiar incidences that determine the predictability or not of the environment in which the decision is to be made.

- *Response Consistency*—i.e., the consistency with which the leader follows through the above considerations in the developed decision model while making decisions.

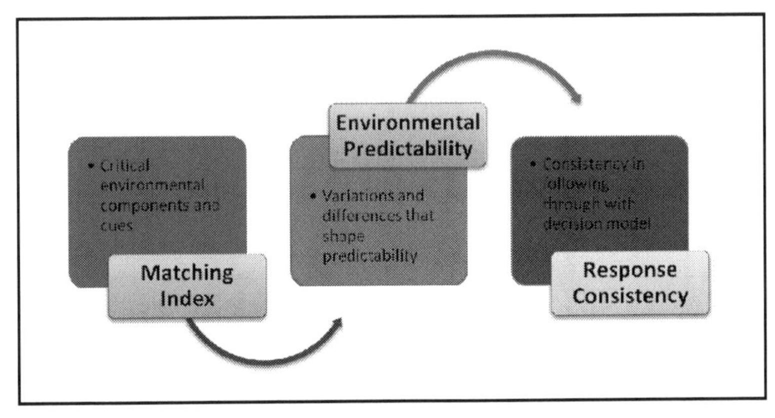

Fig 6.1 Components of a Good Decision-Making Model

When response consistency is diminished, managerial decisions are erratic and less effective. This is why leaders should develop an adaptive decision model that eliminates response inconsistency and enhances the decision-making process.

Managerial Inconsistency as a Function of Poor Metacognition

Earlier in Chapter Four of this book, reference was made to the importance of the cognitive abilities and processes that a leader engages in providing leadership in an organization. Apart from the fact that inconsistency in managerial practices could be due to the inherent character flaws and skill deficiencies of a mediocre leader, it could also flow from inadequacy or deficiency in engaging metacognitive processes. Metacognition is the ability to reflect on, understand and gain effective control of your cognitive assessments in relation to a concrete goal or objective (Flavell, 1976:232; Schraw and Dennison, 1994:460). It helps the leader gain an understanding of the details in given situations vis-à-vis the leader's own cognition. It is valuable in the elimination of erroneous beliefs, defective thinking patterns, and inadequate awareness of the leader's own decision-making process. Metacognition enables leaders to generate multiple decision-making frameworks that focus on interpreting, planning, and implementing goals. A person is said to have a metacognitive experience when in order to comprehend a difficult task, recourse is made to a past experience with a similar difficulty so as to generate a decision framework for resolving this new but identical task (Haynie and Shepherd, 2009:699).

Leaders are able to make sense of a given situation and engage the right decision-making procedure when they can relate the situation to a previous metacognitive experience and apply the same pattern of successful mental processes they had previously employed to gain mastery over the initial experience. This system also helps them improve their metacognitive application as they are better able to delineate successful processes, identify modifications, and incorporate improvements along the way. This level of metacognition reduces the incidences of leaders making erratic and inconsistent strategy decisions. They are able to draw from past experiences, assess their own cognition of the problem or situation, align with an effective decision model, and, where necessary, adapt their decisions to new realities in their environment. In simpler terms, metacognition involves mental processes that gain cognition of current situations by relating them to previous ones, identifying what decision model should be adopted in the decision-making process, and adapting decisions to the perception of current realities in the environment. This helps leaders on two vital levels (Mitchell, Shepherd, & Sharfman, 2011):

(i) It helps them assess their own thinking and process their own understanding of the situation.

(ii) It helps their perception of the external environment and how this affects their thinking.

Due to the cognitive control that effective leaders gain through metacognition, they can maintain consistency in their management decisions, especially in the area of strategic inputs and outcomes. It also helps leaders verify how useful their decision-making processes are so that they can make relevant adjustments. However, mediocre leaders do not engage this level of metacognitive depth. They refuse to generate decision models while tackling complex situations, which could have helped them build a wealth of metacognitive experiences from which they can draw when future occasions demand. Apart from cognition-related complexities, there are two observable mediating factors that influence managerial inconsistencies in decision-making, and they are:

(a) **Environmental Hostility:** Research shows that leaders who have to make management decisions in hostile environ-ments are prone to making erratic decisions than those who operate within less hostile environments (Mitchell, Shepherd, & Sharfman, 2011). Leaders with mediocre skills and who do not engage in metacognition will have a hard time functioning in hostile environments and will more frequently find themselves discomfited. Even for strong leaders, hostility as an intervening factor within the leader's environment increases the tendency to make erratic decisions because of the tense, and in many cases, pressurized nature of the environment. This is because responses to threats or hostile actions from the environment and other forms of urgencies have the likelihood to disrupt information processing. Disruption of information processing disconnects leaders from metacognition and pushes them into spontaneous actions that are outside of any established decision model.

(b) **Environmental Dynamism:** The uncertain and constantly changing nature of an environment makes it dynamic and also increases the pace at which leaders need to make decisions. This creates situations in which they could be erratic in their decision-making. The leader's anxiety about uncertainties and constantly evolving dynamics, especially if they combine with environmental hostilities, can lead to an inability on the part of the leader to make thoughtful choices, which then culminate in strategic decisions that are more erratic. However, these erratic tendencies are mitigated by the fact that strong leaders who operate in high dynamic environments develop increased competitive aggressiveness, engage in numerous cognitive activities, and are constantly under pressure to undergo strategy reorientations in order to stay relevant in the environment. This impact of high dynamism mitigates the rate of inconsistent decisions in hostile environments as against leaders who operate in hostile environments but are low in dynamism. This low level of dynamism puts a weak demand on them to develop more cognitive responses to changes in their environment, and so they do not experience the same degree of positive metacognition as those in highly dynamic contexts.

The table below highlights key deductions made from the foregoing. It is important to note that metacognition is a vital tool that mediocre leaders need to cultivate in order to elevate their leadership potentials and function at more significant levels of effectiveness and excellence. Reflections from the points made above show a great need to covet metacognition and to internalize dynamism in the decision-making processes as essential mitigating factors to inconsistency in management decisions.

Table 6.1 Metacognition in Hostile and Dynamic Environments

- Leaders with high metacognitive experiences are less prone to inconsistent or erratic decisions than those with low metacognitive experiences.
- Leaders experiencing greater hostility in their environments will show a propensity for erratic decisions than those experiencing a low level of hostility.
- Leaders in highly dynamic environments are more prone to erratic decisions than those in environments with lower dynamic environments.
- In hostile environments, leaders who are high in dynamism will experience more positive metacognitive experiences than their counterparts that are low in dynamism.

People Pleasers and Mediocre Leadership

While it is important to develop sound people skills and to have a posture of one who is ready to always listen and be engaged, it is important that leaders and managers strike a balance. If having to leave your door open at every spare time you have is your definition of responsive leadership, then the likelihood is that you won't have any spare time at all to do the real work of making strategic projections, reflections, planning, critiquing, and other vital oversight functions. Having to shove your work to overtime hours in the office in order to cover for lost time weakens the quality of your attention and leaves less room for creative freshness and rejuvenation. It is important for leaders to realize the importance of staying on top of high-priority work and scheduling their time in a way that they devote meaningful hours to getting things done, even if it means being unavailable. Redefining qualitative leadership should sufficiently take into account the need to determine what moderate boundaries will suffice as sufficiently engaging, considerate, and fair enough for interactivity with subordinates while ensuring that vital leadership and management functions do not suffer. It is also important to note that if you keep stealing into other priority areas in your private life in order to accommodate excessive impingements on your time as a leader, your work and life imbalance will accumulate and adversely impact your productivity. We have been taught that relational qualities like being helpful, pleasing, attentive, and reliable bring rewards, and this is what essentially makes us yearn for those affirmations that show we are on the right path (Clancy, 2018). Nonetheless, crossing the line isn't a worthy option either, and it is better to know where to draw the line. When mediocre leaders become people-pleasers, they exhibit the following attitudes:

1. *They say yes to every request*: There is a seemingly compulsive desire to offer their services, assistance, or attention every time it is requested and, in many cases, even when it is not requested from them. There is nothing wrong with being willing to help or provide valuable assistance or skills when they are needed, but mediocre leaders find themselves doing this even when they are overloaded with other crucial work and responsibilities. You have to learn to give your subordinates and colleagues responses like 'sorry, I have to go now;' 'sorry I can't help you with that right now, send me

a report by mail, and I will take a look.' Such responses show that you value the priorities of the organization and know the need to strike a healthy balance. This doesn't apply to only mediocre leaders; analysts have identified that highly intelligent and hardworking people also tend to struggle with letting go of control by delegating, and so they soon overwork themselves and are forced to say yes to every request (Saunders, 2012). This brings us to the next point.

2. *They don't delegate and want to do everything:* This isn't a healthy attitude. Leaders and managers must learn to give up control over matters that others can do and stick with those responsibilities that are strictly within their authority purview or capabilities, and that cannot be delegated. Attending to everything steals your precious time, and you don't have much of it! A business leader who is looking to stay ahead in the strategy game can't afford to be stuck with reprogramming the computers or research work that is best done by subject matter experts—even if these things are in the area of the forte of the leader except the leader's involvement is absolutely necessary.

3. *They set unrealistic standards*: Excellence is a virtue worthy of pursuit, but setting standards that are unrealistic will put you in a perpetual cycle of guilt trips that could dampen your energy, esteem, and sense of contribution to the TEAM. One of such unrealistic standards is trying to make everyone like you at all costs! The bad news is that it won't work! Your responsibility is to create the right environment and level playing field for everyone, to engage your people in a supportive manner, to be courteous and considerate in your approach, and to get the job done! Trying to get everyone to like you is tantamount to begging for attention, and this could send a wrong signal that you are deficient in self-esteem.

People are looking up to you, which means you have their attention; what you need is to provide the right example, motivation, and environment that supports productivity, synergy, and innovation—and after that, get down to work!

4. *They seek validation for their self-worth*: As a leader, you are likely going to disappoint people and be disappointed yourself. This is why it is an attribute of weakness to seek validation as proof of your self-worth. Your work, the results you are achieving with your people, and the positive feedback you get should tell you enough about how much value you are contributing. It is actually proper that organizations recognize the inputs of their staff, and that includes you as a leader. As a matter of fact, there is nothing wrong with leaving an organization where your hard work and valuable contributions aren't valued, but it is important to get your self-worth from a healthy self-image. This way, you can find more objective ways to assess your contributions and gauge the appreciation of those you work with without feeling starved when you aren't constantly validated.

5. *They are not real*: Being down-to-earth is an essential quality that every leader needs. There will be times when you have an "off-day" and can't really be there for others, learn how to politely say no. You may actually have time on your hands, but for some reason, you are not in the mood to help or can't take up any other tasks—learn to politely say no, and don't work yourself up thinking someone might feel let-down or get offended. It is important to be real.

Mediocre Leaders Play Favorites

A review of opinions by experts suggests that there is a tendency that a lot of us are guilty of playing favoritism despite how fair we think we are (Knight, 2017). One of the arguments put forward is that our collective lack of self-awareness, especially on how we come across, reinforces the tendency to play favorites. Though this doesn't negate the fact that we naturally are likely to have different levels of relationships with those we work with and for different reasons. Nonetheless, many leaders and managers often harbor unconscious perceptions that can influence their reviews and day-to-day decisions in respect of employees that are under their management (Business Management Daily, 2009). Leaders must learn not to develop a sense of preference for one (or some) employee(s) over another (or others) because this creates an atmosphere that dampens the morale of other members of your staff, leads to dips in productivity, and can become a foundation for organizational dysfunction. Below are some of the signs that mediocre leaders who play favorites display:

1. They spend more time overseeing certain members of staff and are constantly thinking of ways to improve the career standing and opportunities for growth for these employees. If you find yourself thinking this way about an employee or a group of employees, then you are already harboring the traits of favoritism. There could be different reasons for this; it could be because you played an active role in their recruitment and so you feel responsible for them; it could be because you identify that they have similar traits with you and so you naturally gravitate towards them more, or it could even be because of their unique approach and special gifting. Whatever the case is, favoritism creates a blind spot for mediocre leaders and puts the organization at risk when the favorites move on to another organization, aren't available, or aren't able to deliver as they used to for some reason (such as a health condition).

2. They enjoy communicating more with some employees over others. Communication is perhaps the most powerful tool in organization and TEAM management, and it is the primary live wire supplying the required current for the achievement of your goals and objectives. When leaders are defective in their communication or shy away from the responsibility of carrying their subordinates and colleagues along but prefer turning to a few employees for reliability, engagement, and information dissemination, the organization will begin to suffer deformities. The deformities will adversely affect such areas as uniformity in information access, synergy and TEAM morale, knowledge sharing, ideation, and innovation, among other vital elements that keep a TEAM vibrant.

3. They are eager to conduct reviews for some employees than others. It could be that they are afraid to give negative reviews of their favorite employees who have broken certain rules of engagement and are thus looking for ways to shield these employees. In such situations, they prefer evaluating others and try to dodge the favorites. In other instances, it could be that they have developed an aversion or unfavorable stereotype for some employees. It could be because these employees don't fit into the ideal qualities or pictures that they have or because they don't deliver the kind of results that the favorites deliver. In such instances, mediocre leaders display excitement for their favorite employees and are cold towards others. Every staff is different, and with a level playing field, the right atmosphere, and relevant training, people will deliver at their optimum. However, we must realize that some people are simply just more talented than others, but talent is never enough! You need a committed, hardworking, competent, and dynamic TEAM with high morale, but you can't have that if you hype the value of some and downplay the contributions of others.

4. They relax the rules for certain employees. A manager reprimands some members of his TEAM for coming late, and five minutes later calls on one of his favorite staff to give a report only to discover the staff is not even in the meeting. He goes mum or says something like, "he is probably sick or tracking down a major client; I will deal with that later—but meetings are important and must be taken seriously." The staff shows up after the meeting and gets called into the manager's office only to get a slap on the wrist for scheduling a meeting with a remote prospect he considers potentially valuable, at the same time when he is to be at a strategy meeting. These discretionary attitudes keep getting ignored because he is the highest delivering salesperson in the organization.

   What such mediocre managers don't realize is that this super salesman cannot single-handedly deliver the results of all the committed members of the TEAM. More so, by so doing, instead of creating a healthy drive in others to keep scaling new thresholds, they are de-motivating the TEAM. This creates room for employee turnover, a toxic culture of individualism, and besides, your superstar could get a more tempting offer that makes him leave. You must realize that your people are your most valuable asset, so you must learn how to get the best out of them and keep the TEAM spirit alive. That's what gets organizations through rough patches, and you can be sure that your trials are sure to come! If you burn the bridges when you should be building them, you wouldn't have the required synergy, loyalty, and sacrifice at those critical times when you need them.

5. They don't keep track of who is doing what. Leaders, who are sensitive to equity and fairness, often ask themselves questions like "whose turn is it?" They are, for example, aware that last month they nominated certain members of staff for some high-level assign-

ments, and so now they are thinking of giving others a chance and an opportunity to also prove themselves. Apart from the fact that evenly circulating these engagements provides a platform to enhance the competencies and the innovation level of your employees on a broader level, you can be rest assured that those who aren't getting picked are conscious of it. So, keeping a record of those you have engaged with recently and those who haven't had the chance is crucial. In addition, ensuring that you deliberately give recognition to your employees for their hard work, TEAMwork, individual contributions, and successes is important. Every contribution is significant and should be appreciated.

Micromanagement as an Attribute of Mediocre Leadership

Micromanagement is not a new trait and has been conceptually discussed for many years under different headings. It is commonly described as exercising control over (or within) an organization in every particular and to the smallest detail, with the likely effect of obstructing progress and neglecting broader and higher-level policy issues (White, 2010: p.71). It is the act of trying to personally control and manage everyone/everything in a TEAM or organization in order to control the outcomes in a preferred direction. It reflects a compulsive and behavioral addiction similar to other addictive disorders and is often associated with self-doubt or feeling unsure of others in relation to the achievement of set goals and objectives. Putting the best foot forward in order to curb micromanagement requires that it is first recognized and its attributes identified; only then can a leader take steps to curb his own excesses and allow subordinates more leeway and modest independence to do their jobs. The following are some of the attributes of micromanagers:

1. **They are pathological controllers:** Micromanagers have an obsessive desire to get involved in every detail, to oversee every activity, and to meddle in how their subordinates get the job done. There is nothing wrong with paying attention to details, especially when they concern critical areas of the business; however, excellent managers and leaders know how to use micro-indicators to determine when there are problems and where such problems are emanating from. They design monitoring plans for each project as a way of tracking performance, responding to problem spots, and keeping their eyes on vital details and tasks that are non-delegable due to their sensitive nature. This is a whole world of difference from micromanagement because, at this level, employees are allowed to do their jobs with some measure of independence and are only held accountable to particular standards with necessary oversight to ensure they deliver the goods. This encourages sustainable productivity, creativity, innovation, and morale boost for employees contrary to the long-term debilitating effects of micromanagement, even though it may seem to have immediate benefits.

2. **They are condescending to their staff:** Micromanagers often make their employees feel inadequate and not good enough. They complain all the time and stand over the shoulders of their staff as a way of reminding these employees that they are not trusted or competent. Surprisingly this overdrive may be fueled by the fear of the leader who doesn't want to fail or might be due to insecurity because they always want to prove to their subordinates how competent they are. When a leader is always trying to prove he knows practically everything or that he doesn't have any skill deficiency, the result is that he develops a condescending posture.

3. **They don't accept responsibility for their mistakes:** Due to their compulsive behavior, micromanagers soon take up too many responsibilities, have a lot of files to treat, and have to make a thousand decisions over both serious and mundane matters. This stretches them thin and puts them in a situation in which they are prone to mistakes—not wanting to feel exposed or seem incompetent, they turn around to blame others for their own mistakes and refuse to accept responsibility. This attitude also spills over into concerns with accountability because of the larger-than-life image that they portray, which also makes it more awkward to acknowledge their mistakes.

4. **They don't develop people:** Micromanagers are sometimes highly skilled and efficient people, but rather than train their subordinates and enhance the capabilities of their staff for greater productivity; they instead arrogate to themselves the task of scrutinizing, correcting, and dictating the nitty-gritty of methods, modalities, and technical inputs on various assignments. This bogs down their time and gets them enmeshed in laborious engagements that could have been prevented if they simply organized a relevant curriculum of training for their staff.

5. **They are afraid of competition:** Mediocrity steps in when leaders cannot stand the intelligence, talent, and skills of others. They become manipulative, preferring to control the process of achieving results rather than inspiring their TEAM members to be creative and innovative. Thus, they rarely hire people who they perceive as too talented, skilled, or experienced for them to manipulate and control and would rather hire stereotyped workers who are not a threat to them. This badly hurts the organization, making it settle for a

mediocre skill pool and culture and putting it on a downward spiral in terms of competence, morale, and achievements.

CHAPTER SEVEN

NARROWLY RESTRICTED OUTLOOK

"Nothing limits intelligence more than ignorance; nothing fosters ignorance more than one's own opinions; nothing strengthens opinions more than refusing to look at reality."
—Sheri S. Tepper

Case Study: Enron

In 1985, Enron was established following a merger between Houston Natural Gas Company and Omaha-based InterNorth Incorporated. After the merger, Kenneth Lay, who was once the chief executive officer (CEO) of Houston Natural Gas, was made Enron's CEO and chairman. Lay rebranded Enron into an energy trader and supplier. With the deregulation of the energy markets, companies could place bets on future prices, and Enron took advantage of this. In 1990, Lay created the Enron Finance Corporation, appointing Jeffrey Skilling, whose work as a McKinsey & Company consultant had impressed Lay. This made Lay choose him to be in charge of the new corporation. He joined Enron at a favorable time when the minimal regulatory environment enabled Enron to flourish. However, the flourishing soon ended due to some poorly made decisions.

The story of Enron Corporation shows how a company that reached dramatic heights could soon face a shocking fall. The company's collapse affected thousands of employees and deeply shook Wall Street. At Enron's peak, its shares were worth about $90.75; just before declaring bankruptcy on December 2, 2001, they were trading at twenty-six cents. To this day, many wonder how such a robust business, which at the time was one of the largest companies in the United States, disintegrated almost overnight. It is also difficult to fathom how its leadership managed to fool regulators for so long with fake holdings and off-the-books accounting.

The collapse was such a great fall that it became popular to describe companies that fall from their formidable or indomitable positions as "doing an Enron." Enron went from $100 billion in "revenue" and 29,000 employees at the beginning of 2001 to file for bankruptcy at the end of the same year. The $63.4 billion Enron had tied up in assets made it the largest corporate bankruptcy in American history until WorldCom's bankruptcy in 2002.

It turns out that Enron's executives were using accounting loopholes, unique purpose entities, and false error reporting to hide billions of dollars of debt from failed deals and projects. If they built a power plant and it was expected to make $2 billion in revenue, that was what was reported, rather than the money it actually made. Enron's executives did not just mislead the board of directors; they also pressured their auditors to shred, delete, and hide any evidence.

Enron's management fooled regulators with fake holdings and off-the-books accounting practices. The company used special purpose vehicles (SPVs), or special purposes entities (SPEs), to hide its mountainous debt and toxic assets from various investors and creditors. The company was forced to pay its creditors more than $21.7 billion from 2004 to 2011.

One of the indispensable assets a leader needs is the ability to see the big picture. Interestingly this requires that leaders have some measure of discipline, awareness, and open-mindedness in order to closely observe the world around them and take in a wider scope and deeper understanding of the internal and external environments in which they operate. This discipline of deliberate awareness and open-mindedness makes them observant of trends, changes, opportunities, trouble spots, and the likely problems that the organization is facing or will face, both from an internal and external perspective. Such leaders are also able to process their observations and thus determine what positive or negative impacts the unfolding trends, opportunities, or problems could have on the business on a short-term or long-term basis. For leaders to operate from such broad-based and up-to-date perspectives, they must be open-minded, interact reflectively with their environment, pay impartial attention to changes around them, and diligently process the information and feelers they get for the strategic good of the organization.

Closed-minded and mediocre leaders do not do much to be a part of their environment and the evolving trends that define the world in which they live and do business. Their point of view to issues often follows a narrow one-way course that is essentially oblivious to:

- The dynamics and necessities of the times and how their organizations are faring internally and externally based on emerging trends.

- The need to constantly assess the state of their internal workflow, systems, and culture for their overall health, for weak or trouble spots, for areas of strength, and for opportunities for leverage.

- The imperative for strategic positioning helps the organization identify and respond to business threats in the environment, and that also helps it to recognize and seize opportunities.

- The limitedness of their thinking. They do not see value in the concerns, insights, suggestions, and alternative ideas of their subordinates, TEAM members, experts, and/or stakeholders. They are fixated on their opinions and do not entertain opposing debates, contrary opinions, or different ideas.

- Their personal state of cultural unfitness and dissonance.

These leaders are not able to sense the winds of change or spot potential storms that lie ahead. They also have difficulty seeing new pathways and patterns that could open new vistas of opportunities for them and their organizations. When organizations portray a narrow outlook in their operations and business outcomes, it is primarily due to the closed-minded posture of their leadership. Sometimes, being open-minded simply requires developing a mental discipline to being mindful, informed, and impartial about happenings that may have wider or long-term implications. It also includes being deliberately tolerant and open to broader scopes of assessments when solving problems, evaluating decisions, dealing with change, or tackling current business issues (Stephanie Mead, 2020). At other times it requires that leaders take a break from the routine demands on their time and energy and redirect such time and energy to do some extensive research and consultations; think deeply about the pros, cons, and different ideas they come across; and take action based on the holistic picture that they have gained of the situation and the potential ramifications of their decisions.

One common example of a narrowly restricted outlook to business leadership and management is the short-term gratification that many executives gain from inflating their earnings by cutting down on their expenditure. While it must be stated categorically that cutting down on irrelevant expenses and finding more cost-effective ways to achieving the same or better results is a crucial quality of excellent management and leadership, however, projecting impressions of improved earnings instead of a reduction in cost is surely a myopic reliance to determine an increase in the value of a company's stock. This is because such inflated figures may not be a true reflection of the company's response to market needs and demands; neither do they usually reflect improved sales or service delivery. As a result of this, even if the stock value improves due to greater investor evaluation, there is likely no solid sustainability model to underpin performance and growth. As a matter of fact, the initial cuts in expenditure may be too discretionary and could have long-term adverse impacts on performance, while the absence of an actual market-oriented growth strategy soon becomes obvious, leading to eventual stagnation and decline in the stock value of the company within a short time. The problem here is the narrow interpretation the leader attaches to the significance of cutting down costs, without a proper evaluation of possible long-term impacts of cuts in crucial areas and a well-thought-out growth strategy that is responsive to market opportunities and realities.

In the light of the above illustration, while a wider profit margin due to cost management is, in fact, healthy for any organization and commendable; however, relying solely on this to boost a company's stock value is a narrow-minded approach to facilitating a company's growth. Without a mindful, impartial, and open-minded process of distilling relevant information, evaluating different ideas, and engaging a thorough process of weighing the pros and cons of viable business opportunities and modifications, such a process might yield immediate fruit but will reach a standstill and eventual decline soon enough. A study involving 2,859 companies showed that businesses that made unwise cuts to expenses in order to artificially project better performance during their equity issue ended up losing profits in the long run and causing their stock value to dip by as much as 20% within four years (Mizik and Jacobson, 2007). The important point here is that leaders should engage an open mind and a broad-based perspective to their decision-making and leadership. Narrow organizational outlooks and patterns of results, on the other hand, are characteristic of mediocre leadership because, just as we have seen in the survey mentioned, the narrow perspective of leaders can inhibit the long-term potentials of organizations and can be evidence of a closed-minded approach to leadership. This closed-mindedness becomes the albatross and limitation to the leader's potentials and that of the organization. Therefore, a narrow organizational outlook or paradigm is essentially a reflection of closed-minded leadership.

What is Closed-Mindedness?

Rigidity is one of the weaknesses that mediocre leaders have, but over the years, psychologists have made several attempts to distinguish between rigidity and closed-mindedness as two distinct mental states that individuals could exhibit. They could easily be mistaken as the same, but the distinctions made by experts have shown that there is a clear point of difference between them that better helps us to put them in proper perspective. In identifying how a closed mind works, we can describe the process as dogmatic thinking that is walled within a total cognitive system of ideas and beliefs that are rooted in relatively impermeable, impenetrable, or restricted ideological leanings (Montgomery, 1972). This means that dogmatic or closed-minded leaders operate within an encompassing system of thinking and cognition that is influenced by certain closed systems of ideas, ideals, creeds, beliefs, and persuasions. This closed system of ideals and beliefs suggests that in relation to specific issues, the dogmatic views are stubbornly resistant to change even when there are logical arguments or objective evidence that disprove the credibility of the ideological dispositions.

Experts have also established that closed-minded or dogmatic people are generally resistant to change, with the exception that they only change when a recognized authority changes or requests for change (Rokeach, 1954, 1960; Rokeach, McGavney, and Denny 1955, 1960). Experts have, therefore, situated the understanding of closed-mindedness within the parameters of dogmatism, pointing out that a closed mind is essentially one that is dogmatic in its inclination and outlook (Montgomery, 1972). The difference between dogmatism and rigidity is that dogmatism (i.e., closed-mindedness) is a higher-order and more complex form of resistance to change. Dogmatism also reflects a total cognitive configuration of a relatively closed system of ideas and beliefs. Rigidity, on the other hand, deals more with difficulties in overcoming single sets of approaches to tackling specific tasks or problems. It can be described as an isolated way(s) in which a person attacks, solves, or learns specific tasks or problems. Rigidity is the difficulty or inability to communicate between neighboring cognitive regions (i.e., the pre-ideological/ primitive, intermediate, or peripheral regions) in a way that makes it hard to adapt different approaches, experiences, ideas, and beliefs.

The pre-ideological region of beliefs refers to those daily beliefs that we take for granted, from which some of our other beliefs and perceptions take their cue. They are formed based on our understanding of physical reality, social reality, and the nature of the self (i.e., the individual) in the world we live in. These are generally undisputed beliefs about what is or what exists—such as believing that a couple is one's parents, or that a kind of solid material is wood and is for making furniture, or what one's name is. Secondly, the intermediate region of beliefs refers to the beliefs that are formed based on the perceptions people have in or about the different nature of authorities in their environment and what authority or authorities they line up with or join others to line up with. The authorities relied upon differ from person to person depending on the nature of their experiences and social structure; besides, the particular authorities relied upon determine how people perceive and interpret the world in which they live. Through the social influences of these authorities, people develop cognitive conceptions of what to trust and align with and what to distrust and stay away from.

The third and final region is the peripheral region of beliefs which has two streams, i.e., derived beliefs and inconsequential beliefs. Derived peripheral beliefs are beliefs concerning matters of fact that are held primarily because we trust authoritative sources such as texts and reference books or other recognized authorities (Rokeach, 1960). Inconsequential peripheral beliefs are beliefs of personal taste that come from a direct encounter with the object of belief, and such beliefs do not require social consensus for their maintenance. For instance, the preference for homemade cookies instead of the assorted ones from the store may be based on the belief that homemade cookies are tastier, but this is a matter of personal taste and preference and doesn't require social consensus.

Furthermore, there are certain characteristics that help delineate between dogmatism and rigidity. One of which is that closed-minded and dogmatic people have difficulties integrating or synthesizing new beliefs or ideas that contradict their prior beliefs or persuasions. The difficulty is premised on the fact that they are unwilling to play along or entertain new belief systems—except those initiated by a recognized authority—because these new ideas greatly threaten the foundational coherence of a closed-minded person. A closed-minded person may also have difficulty in even recalling the new information or belief that is to be integrated because of the unwillingness to accommodate it in the first place. Hence, their cognition is based on a closed system of beliefs and principles that tend to ward off new thoughts or ideas that are divergent or that differ from their hitherto held beliefs.

Meanwhile, the degree of rigidity a person may exhibit is essentially in respect to analysis and not about synthesis or the integration of new ideas. It is majorly about their ability to process or interpret new ideas in a way that they find useful or advantageous and thus become willing to adopt them. This is why though dogmatism may lead to rigidity in how specific problems are solved; it doesn't necessarily follow that the converse is the case (Montgomery, 1972)—i.e., people may be rigid but may not be dogmatic. Rigidity applies more as a response in person-to-thing situations, where a person's difficulties are essentially about analyzing new approaches and nothing personal, but dogmas have a tint of being personal and apply more in person-to-person situations (Rokeach, 1954). The table below captures some of the key differences between dogmatism/closed-mindedness and rigidity.

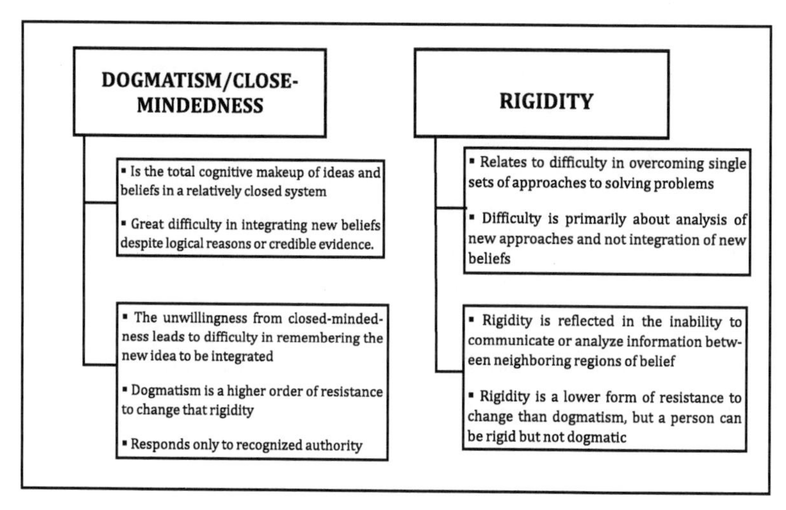

Fig 7.1 Some Major Differences between Dogmatism/Closed-mindedness and Rigidity

Insular Leadership

Insular leadership is a situation in which a leader and some followers downplay or disregard the interests and welfare of those outside their group, organization, or those they are immediately responsible for. Kellerman (2014) describes it as a situation in which the "...leader and at least some followers minimize or disregard the health and welfare of 'the other'— that is, those outside the group or organization for which they are directly responsible." They establish a demarcation that separates them from every other person not captured within their immediate constituency or catchment of relations and turn a blind eye to problems or challenges that do not have a direct bearing on their immediate interests and the interests of those within their group. Closed-minded people often exhibit this tendency to be more interested in the events, happenings, or even tragedies that befall those within their group or network of affiliations, while they show a cold or indifferent interest in what happens to others. This is not always the result of a callous mind—though in many cases it is—but could be as a result of a narrow focus and fixated attention on a limited set of interests, such that they become oblivious, unaware and dull in their sensitivity towards "other" happenings in their environment.

Insulation in itself isn't an entirely bad idea. This is because, to a certain degree, it is natural for us to feel a greater sense of responsibility for those in our immediate circle, like members of our family, TEAM members, members of staff, or people within a group we share some sort of affiliation with. Due to this sense of obligation, we might tend to be protective and to seek out the interests of those in these circles above those of others. However, turning a blind eye and doing nothing about the dangers and tragedies that befall "other" people not captured within our immediate circles, in the end, has a greater cost and implication than what it would have cost to doing something initially. The interconnectedness of events in our world is far proving that it is more difficult to turn a blind eye to the tragedies of others and not be inadvertently sowing or watering a seed that will soon come to haunt us.

Steven Ibbotson (2018)— an academy teacher and a leader with several years of leadership experience in religious organizations and on the board of several non-profits—provides us with an interesting perspective on insularity that helps us to contextualize it from an organizational standpoint. He describes an insular organization as "...one that has few (if any) sources of new knowledge, ideas or resources." As has been noted already, insulation in itself is not entirely a bad idea. As Ibbotson (2018) observes, most companies like to incorporate some level of "insulation" into their policies in order to keep out undesirable people, habits, or views from their business. In the same manner, good organizations like to keep the valuable resources they have—human, financial, and otherwise—from leaving, and thus have an insulation policy that shields them from losing such valuable resources. Notwithstanding, every organization, just like a house, needs both insulation and ventilation. Doors and windows that are open are the primary ways through which ventilation enters a house. In like manner, leaders and their organizations need a "ventilation" system through which new knowledge, ideas, and people enter the organization, and as an opening for others who no longer fit in to leave the company —either voluntarily or by showing them the way out when it becomes necessary. The emphasis in this particular organizational ventilation is on the "new," i.e., it is important that there are opportunities for new and fresh knowledge, ideas, people, and resources to come in.

When leaders are insular because they turn a blind eye to the tragedies of "others," they create a blind spot in their leadership and develop an insensitivity that makes them oblivious to happenings in their environments; these happenings eventually boomerang in escalated proportions in a manner that comes back to haunt them. In the other sense, when leaders make their organizations insular by not creating ventilation systems that help to bring new ideas and hands on board, the organization becomes stale and begins to lose relevance until it finally dies out. These two illustrations are depicted in the diagrams below.

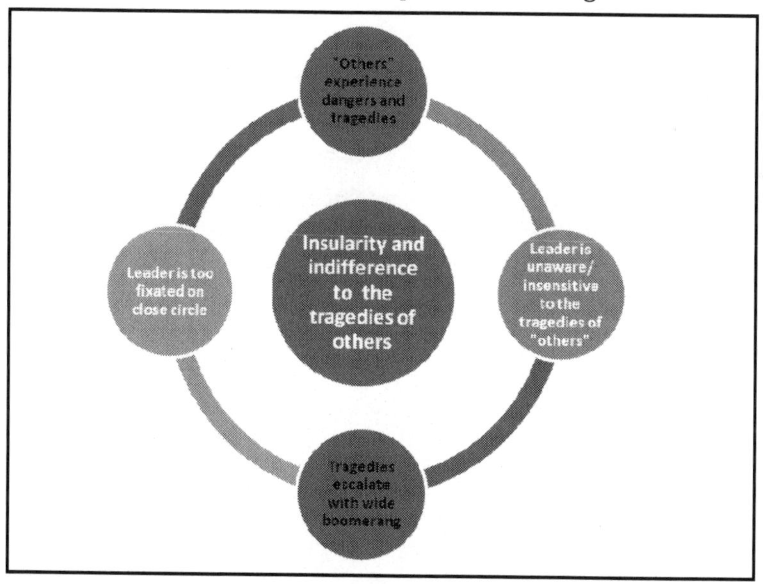

Fig 7.2 Insular Leadership that "Turns the Blind Eye"

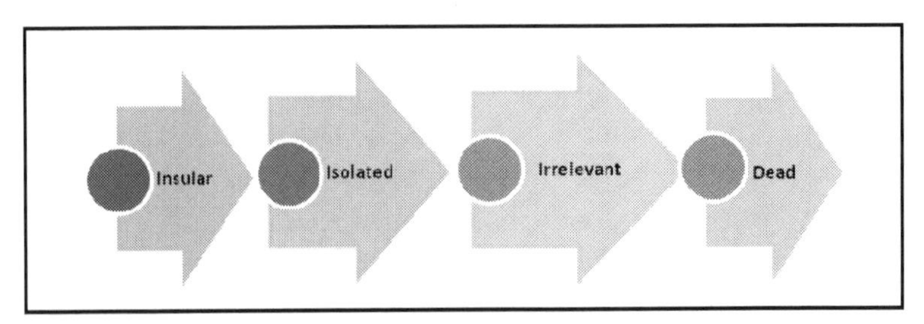

Fig 7.3 An Insular Organization that doesn't "Ventilate"

Cut-off from the Environment

Leaders often find themselves in situations in where they are isolated from their people either because of busy schedules that have kept them on assignments outside of the organization or because some sort of distance has developed between these leaders, their key point men, and by extension, other members of staff. Mediocre leaders often dwell in the second realm and get caught up in an unhealthy isolated situation that cuts them off from the pulse of the workplace. A leader's deliberate engagement with subordinates and members of the TEAM is important to maintaining up-to-date awareness of happenings in the work environment. Isolated leaders, due to their poor orientation and weak interpersonal skills, often find themselves creating chasms through corporate structures that are oriented along top-down communication, hierarchical silos, absence of employer-employee interface, and a lack of trust between n management and field staff (FMI, 2010).

These leaders are often trapped in an executive or management bubble of invincibility, pride, over-optimism, and impaired perception of realities. The major result of this isolation is that these leaders only get organizational information that has been filtered on many levels, seriously streamlined, and analytically repackaged, putting them at the receiving end of stale or distorted information. This puts the organization at risk because the leader isn't able to spot problems until they have become quite endemic, threatening, or costly. This also comes from a lopsided leadership approach that is centered on achieving business results but isn't inclined towards properly catering to the needs of the TEAM and nurturing it to reach its highest potentials. Analysts report that when leaders disengage, isolate, and cut themselves off from the TEAM and work environment, employees begin to feel overlooked, ignored, and condescended to. They feel stifled, and this may lead to loss of creativity, despondency, absenteeism, sabotage, low productivity, and worker attrition (FMI, 2010). Employees who were hitherto motivated may also become dampened in their morale. They may, as a result, resign to doing just the minimum required since they have a sense that their efforts will not be recognized, neither will their opinions count for a change. In extreme cases, this can lead to loss of valuable human capital through employee turnover.

Effective leaders know the importance of engagement both within their internal environment (i.e., with employees and TEAM members) and also with the realities of the market (i.e., with customers, various links in the value chain, and industry experts).

Not Recognizing Bad Outcomes

The narrow-minded nature of mediocre leaders is also reflected in their inability to recognize bad outcomes because they believe they are always right and have a microscopic view of the impact of their subpar leadership. While historically, emphasis on leadership qualities seem to have focused more on the valiance and successes of great leaders, who eventually became prototypes for leadership studies due to their great feats; today, however, a significant focus of studies by experts in business analyses is geared towards unraveling the mysteries and miseries that occasion ineffective and average scale leadership. For instance, it has been noted that the actions of ineffective leaders usually become a burden that land on their subordinates, which then fall on the company, and finally come full circle fall on the leaders themselves (Aboyassin and Abood, 2013: p.69). This suggests that everyone in the chain pays for ineffective and narrow-minded leadership, whether it is the subordinates, the company/organization itself, or the narrow-minded leaders themselves—everyone suffers the consequence. If mediocre leaders can understand this important viewpoint, their attitudes to leadership will probably take a turn for the better, and this will help them appropriate proactive measures that can upgrade their leadership skills, methods and help improve the outcomes they get. Narrow-minded leadership can play negative roles in de-motivating employees and making a negative impact on individual and organizational productivity. As has been earlier discussed in this book, mediocre leadership has an unethical side, but it is also important to note that it has a dimension of ineffectiveness to it.

It is important to opine at this point that when we talk about great leaders or great leadership systems and methods, our focus is often on the observable outcomes, impacts, or effects that such leadership makes on an organization over a given period or at a specific point in time. This means that our assessment of qualitative leadership is significantly moderated by the quality of effects such style of leadership is able to make on the major indices of leadership that we consider critical to success in our organizations. Thus, effectiveness (whether in meeting organizational goals, scaling the business, efficiently managing financial, material, and human resources, or increasing business success through innovation) is a crucial parameter for determining the quality of leadership being provided. Therefore, mediocre/narrow-minded leadership can be said to be designated as such due to the weaknesses it exhibits in terms of effects, results, and impact compared to those of excellent leadership. Every organization must determine what particular leadership qualities and outcomes are important to it, but there are general measures for assessing qualitative leadership. Leaders must be able to mobilize people towards the achievement of set goals, objectives, and the organization's vision and mission statements. As W.C.H Prentice puts it: "Leadership is the accomplishment of a goal through the direction of human assistants, and the man who successfully marshals his human collaborators to achieve particular ends is a leader; while a great leader is one who can do so day after day, and year after year, in a wide variety of circumstances."

Instructively, there are dynamics of leadership that relate to either the art or the science of it. For instance, an analysis of the Emerging Leadership Theory (ELT) notes that the first dimension of leadership is to build a foundation using the four pillars (4 Cs) of leadership: i.e., character, culture, communication, and charisma; while the second dimension is to keep developing the various emerging skills needed to lead an organization by constantly learning, unlearning and relearning within the context of empirical observations, experimentations, and available data in the industry. The first dimension relates more to the art of leadership, while the second dimension relates more to the science of it. From a holistic standpoint, the level of effectiveness a leader possesses in these two overarching dimensions of leadership is indispensable to determining the quality of leadership being offered. These two areas are often further broken down into various forms of assessments or lists of specific qualities in order to measure effectiveness. When a leader's views, skills, and methods do not sufficiently reflect the required build to fit into these broad-based dimensions and specific qualities, it shows a deeper problem of a narrow-minded configuration. The aggregate degree of exhibited effectiveness or ineffectiveness in the various indices being evaluated becomes the defining mark of the quality of leadership being offered—i.e., whether excellent, mediocre, or poor.

This means that the extent of leadership effectiveness determines whether a person is an excellent, mediocre, or poor leader, and ineffective leadership is necessarily an offspring of the existing narrow perspective and build of the leader. It could also be a result of an emerging attribute of narrow thinking and shrinking perspective. As already mentioned above, using the available body of knowledge on leadership and based on specific corporate and industry needs, organizations need to develop their own yardstick for measuring effectiveness and ineffectiveness; and they also should envisage what the likely adverse nature of narrow and ineffective leadership could be in order to better recognize and nip it in the bud.

For instance, in a 2013 study on the effects of ineffective leadership on Jordanian institutions, four parameters were adopted in measuring ineffectiveness: i.e., lack of shared strategic vision; ineffective leadership characteristics (such as putting self-interest above the organization, taking advantage of workers, etc.); negative effects on labor relations; and ethical violations (Aboyassin and Abood, 2013). The negative outcomes of such narrow frames of leadership attributes are bound to adversely impact the fortunes of a company to the point that its survival may be dependent on the leader's exit. In the cited study, three of the four dimensions were observed to have the most significant negative impact on the organizational performance of the institutions under evaluation, and they were lack of shared strategic vision, negative effect on labor relationships, and lack of ethics.

Using some other measures of assessments, narrow-minded leadership could be exhibited through the toxic and short-sighted orientation of leaders. In this context, these leaders become known for making hasty decisions and changing course abruptly, which is a consequence of their defective thinking because they wait until there is a last-minute crisis before making vital decisions. This limits the quality of inputs in strategic engagement, if any, and shortens the quality of time that could have been devoted to planning. Since these leaders mount pressure for delivery, employees often find themselves pulled in different directions, leading to situations of confusion and panic. Toxic leaders and managers compromise organizational morale, interfere with information sharing and cooperation, affect talent retention, and are unpredictable. They are focused only on immediate fast-paced goals and budget-driven considerations that they leave little or no room for feedback and innovation (Appelbaum & Roy-Girard, 2007).

As we have seen with major corporate scandals like the Nortel and Enron scandals and the 2008 global economic crisis, short-sighted leaders often do not connect their lack of foresight and narrow thinking to the possible destruction of the company or other severe impacts on its corporate wellbeing. The report on Enron's CEO, Jeffrey Skilling, who in the bid to meet his target of lofty earnings mistreated his employees and derided those who didn't seize the moment to be "creative" in meeting targets at all cost, showed that this created a culture of greed in the firm (Appelbaum & Roy-Girard, 2007: p.20). In the end, the perpetual chaos, cycles of abrupt reorganizations, and undisciplined spending caused an implosion in the organization. At the peak of his reign, Skilling most likely didn't consider the holistic and long-term implications of his actions, just like Andrew Fastow, Enron's CFO, who bullied employees into performing illegal accounting procedures until the situation became a scandal. Such narrow approaches to problem-solving and goal achievement have grave repercussions for the organization in the long term, a fact that narrow-minded leaders often ignore. These negative repercussions could also apply to regular non-scandalous situations in which narrow-minded leaders do not act with the big picture in mind. They become insensitive to the undermining effect that their narrow thinking could have on the level of productivity, corporate culture, and general outcomes of the organization.

Culturally Unaware

The discussion under this subheading is a clarion call to 21st Century leaders on the pivotal significance of mastering the skill of cultural interpretation in what has been aptly described as a 21st Century cultural milieu that is utterly unpredictable, almost totally opaque, empowered, uncontrollable, and even chaotic (Zammit-Lucia, 2015). Business sustainability is becoming more closely tied to the apron strings of social sensitivity, relevance, and responsibility. It is an environment in which mediocrity, cultural illiteracy, and socio-cultural unawareness have become quicksand that organizations must do everything to avoid; otherwise, they begin to sink. It looks more like leaders whose businesses and organizations will survive and then thrive within the 21st Century's social construct must learn a cultural leadership approach that prioritizes the connection and interrelationships that exist between an organization and the cultural environment in which it operates. The value of observing emerging socio-cultural trends cannot be overemphasized, but the concern is that the conservative, narrow, and indifferent disposition of mediocre leaders can be a huge deficit and burden on the neck of nascent or struggling organizations.

There is a substantial growing shift in how leaders view their roles and in their awareness of the complex social issues that exist in the world in which they do business. This growing shift not only factors in the importance of business survival, growth, and obligations to shareholders but also extends to the public perception of the business decisions of corporate leaders and the ramifications of the social or communal impact of such decisions. As a matter of fact, some analysts and experts have opined that the importance of organizational strategy in leadership should now take a secondary order of priority, while higher considerations such as purpose, values, beliefs, emotions, ethics, and other such vital intangibles, should take the front seat (Zammit-Lucia, 2015: p. 12). Our position on this is that business leaders owe their organizations the sense to remain adaptable to changing socio-cultural trends and to designing their strategies on a short-term basis while pursuing their long-term visions. The long-term goals and health of the organization must fundamentally be in view and should be the drive for maintaining workable short-term strategies that are sensitive to the times.

Unfortunately, mediocre leaders tend to already have a microscopic view of things even when they observe them from the platform of their organizational interests. They are, therefore, in much more difficult straits when it comes to viewing their organizations from these external social perceptions that are in constant metamorphosis. It is crucial to state that looking at the organization from the outside has become of critical importance to leaders who want to succeed in today's near topsy-turvy social environment. This is preferable to the practice of having the interpretation of the culture and society in which we operate as businesses presented to us through several filters. Such filters include our own organizational lens, opinions of people who are most like us, theories from our institutions and ivory towers, and information from professional associations, among others. On the contrary, catching a good glimpse of how our organizations are perceived by regular people (who are the potential customers, clients, and trend influencers) has become crucial to sustainability.

It is becoming increasingly obvious that the restricted conceptions of economists in explaining market behavior have gone beyond the "rational" doctrine to unpredictable, ambiguous, and revolutionary realities. Getting otherwise narrow-minded leaders who cannot operate from such a big picture and dynamic outlook (i.e., the ability to look from the inside and also from the outside) is likely to snowball into an intractable problem. The diagram below juxtaposes what should be the differences in cultural leadership approach between the 20th and 21st Centuries.

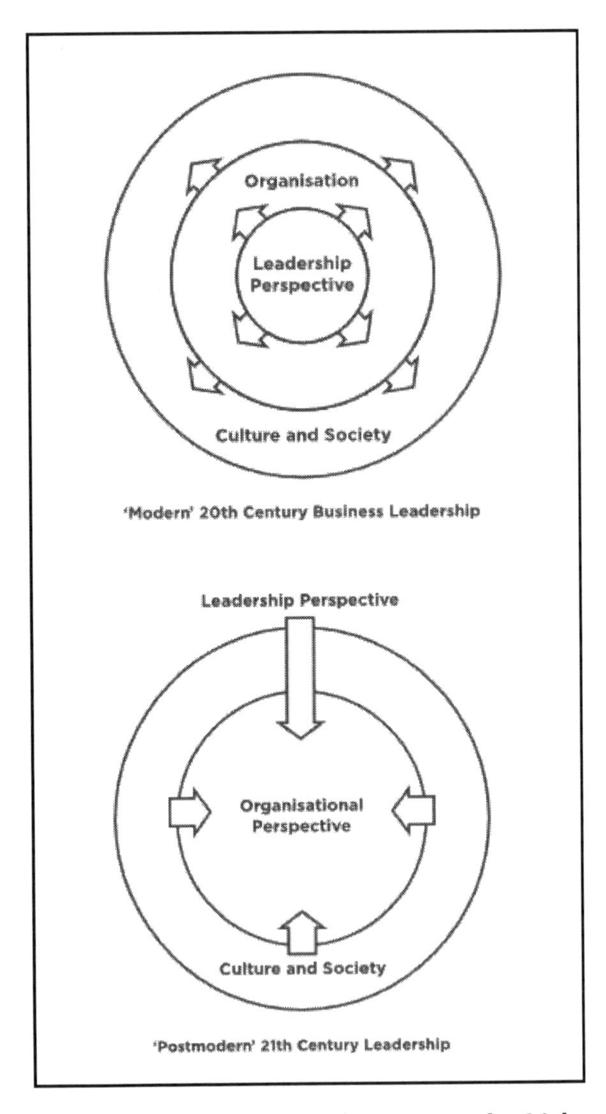

Fig 7.4 Cultural Leadership Differences in the 20th and 21st Centuries (Zammit-Lucia, 2015: p.13)

CHAPTER EIGHT

SELF-CENTERED CHARACTERISTICS "I" OVER "WE"

"We have self-centered minds, which get us into plenty of trouble. If we do not come to understand the error in the way we think, our self-awareness, which is our greatest blessing, is also our downfall!"
—Joko Beck

Case Study: Powa

There are some notable failures in the tech industry that we can learn from, as can be seen in the case of Powa. Powa was one of Britain's brightest tech startups. Once praised by David Cameron and valued at over $1bn (£694m) before floating on a stock market, it was described as a rare British "unicorn."

Hailed as Britain's brightest tech startup, the mobile e-commerce company seemed to be designed for great things. However, in 2016, the company crashed after the founder, Dan Wagner, bragged about a deal with China's UnionPay, which would give them access to more than 1.3 billion customers and trump Apple Pay. Mr. Wagner claimed that the business was worth $2.7bn (£1.9bn) and had signed a deal in China that had "limitless" potential. However, privately, the Powa TEAM that had negotiated the deal was shocked because they suggested that Mr. Wagner not oversell the deal, but he went off-script, not listening to their advice. Powa's PR firm eventually approached the BBC with a story that the company had sealed a fantastic deal in China. They mentioned how PowaTag would gain access to the 1.3 billion customers of China's UnionPay and open up new possibilities for mobile commerce. Unfortunately for Powa, the CEO of UnionPay issued a cease-and-desist letter to Powa and pulled the deal, resulting in the company's demise.

Mr. Wagner, who claimed to be an exceptional serial entrepreneur, always bragged about how his company would be bigger than Google or Facebook. He once told Evan Davis on Radio 4's Bottom Line that the business had been valued at $2.7bn by its backers Wellington. Evan affirmed that it was a meaningless figure because Powa had not made any money yet. The important lesson is that Wagner was so absorbed in himself, his fantasies, and his ambition that he disregarded his TEAM and acted alone. His self-awareness overshadowed any relevance that his TEAM could have been to him on a deal that they were advising wasn't in the best interest of the company.

Although, the fall of Powa may have raised certain questions among analysts about the health of London's much-vaunted fintech sector and what wisdom could be behind making high valuations for unproven businesses. However, Powa is an example of how ego can damage any business. The ego does not necessarily lead to the company's abject failure, but it can lead to consumers turning their backs on the company. The fall of Powa presents a model on how not to run a company. Besides Mr. Wagner's ego, Powa's issues included the problems of no clear strategy, directionless management, overblown claims, and a reckless attitude to money. On the Glassdoor jobs site, which features employees' ratings of companies as places to work, Powa's entry featured a number of reviews criticizing the management, especially the chief executive. One of the reviews read: "You don't employ intelligent, highly experienced people to treat them like something unpleasant under your shoe, by telling them to forget everything they know, as your way isn't working."

There was a time the members of staff received a weird email from Mr. Wagner with the subject line as, "Long live the legacy of David Bowie." The email contained a photo of Mr. Wagner dressed as Ziggy Stardust in full make-up with the caption: "I don't do tributes in half measures!" This mail displeased many employees. According to one of the employees, "While the company was going under, he's fooling around in a photography studio pretending to be Ziggy Stardust. The guy is a narcissistic idiot." Mr. Wagner seemed not to be able to see beyond himself, and this contributed to the fall of Powa.

In the wider context of social consciousness, social scientists and scholars have noted that since the middle of the 20th Century, there appears to have been a growing trend of individualism —especially in the West. It can be seen in the rise of independent people who pursue an individualistic sense of success, fulfillment, and relevance; and also in the declining state of collective identities, culture, and norms. Though individualism has been mostly designated as a predominantly Western trait (i.e., a trait common in Western Europe, North America, and Australia), while collectivism has been linked more to African, Asian and South-American societies (Green, Deschamps & Páez, 2005); these delineations, however, don't change the fact that in leadership and management contexts, leaders and managers who are individualistic, or in adverse cases self-centered, occur across cultures. From a broad scope of the terms individualism and collectivism, we may not strictly define one as negative and the other as positive; notwithstanding this, the preference for a collectivist orientation that accommodates individual uniqueness, but prioritizes group interests and wellbeing, is a pearl of well-established wisdom in leadership and management philosophy.

Individualism in the broad sense of the word is associated with such attributes as independence, self-reliance, autonomy, individual uniqueness, competitiveness, and achievement orientation, among other such qualities. Collectivism, on the other hand, is associated with attributes such as identification with group norms, a sense of duty and obligation to one's group, interdependence, loyalty to group interests, and a desire for social harmony, among others. In narrowing down the discourse on individualism to the effects it could have on leadership, we must interrogate how individualism could interfere with issues like tolerance, willingness to participate, TEAM spirit and solidarity, and other important traits that make great groups,

TEAMs, and societies thrive. Since leadership is about influencing others towards the achievement of specified goals and objectives, it cannot exist in an isolated manner from the group or social contexts. The fundamental interest here is in tracing whether individualism, on the one hand, or collectivism, on the other hand, is better suited to leadership. Self-centered leadership is connotative of an untoward personalization of leadership positions and roles in a way that guarantees pecuniary benefits and personal advancement, while the leader puts up a front or shallow commitment to organizational interests.

The connection between individualist inclination and self-centered leadership is inherent in the individualist's overriding preoccupation with securing the space for personal interests, happiness, and independence; and in the self-centered leader's preoccupation with appropriating the contested space of advancement, with a determination for goals and opportunities that advance overriding self-interests. Both are more focused on their scope of individualized priorities, with underlying dispositions and motivations that could overshadow broader collective concerns, interests, and objectives.

A subtle difference between both streams of individualist pursuit is that the self-centered behavior seems to be an extreme adverse trait of individualistic pursuit. Gustavsson (2007) noted the numerous concerns of communitarians about the negative impact of external individualism on the diminished sense of solidarity (which should be indicative of TEAM spirit) and the reduced sense of community (indicative of cohesion) that might resort from excessive external individualism. Interestingly, the view of libertarians is that those who commit to positive rights (in this sense, the protected rights of people to their autonomy in public participation) could under certain circumstances go to the extent of curtailing the negative rights of others in order to guarantee the protection of the public space for individual participation—which is what they consider to be indispensable for all. Although Gustavsson (2007) examines both views from a broader individualist perspective, the communitarians fight for the collective rights to individual freedom in the public space—which gives them a collectivist inclination. The libertarians are more concerned about the individual's right to privacy away from the public eye or interference.

In reality, there are certain advantages that must come from a healthy dose of individualistic attributes and which may not be found anywhere else, just as there are disadvantages that could result from a misconception and misapplication of collectivism. However, studies show that collectivism has a positive influence on organizational citizenship behaviors, which help to boost synergy, productivity, and performance in organizations (León and Finkelstein, 2011; Dávila & Finkelstein, 2010; Oyserman, Coon, & Kemmelmeier, 2002; Moorman & Blakely, 1995). Organizational citizenship behaviors (OCB) are those employee activities that exceed the formal job roles assigned to employees but which are carried out by committed staff in order to ensure smooth functioning within the organization.

On the other hand, most studies on individualism haven't been able to establish a positive relationship between individualism and OCB. Collectivist traits like sacrificing for the common good, maintaining cordial relations, and helping each other, among others, have been proven to enhance performance, role identity, synergy, and OCB. Meanwhile, individualistic employees have been noted to pursue personal gain as a priority and rule, hence assisting others or the organization only seems attractive to them to the extent that the activity yields personal benefits which cannot be obtained otherwise (León and Finkelstein, 2011). It is this finding that experts consider to be responsible for the lack of positive correlation between individualism and an extraordinary commitment by employees (that is motivated by TEAM spirit).

The Self-Centered Leader

The self-centered leader is that leader whose leadership style in the normal pursuit of the organization's mandate and goals is significantly influenced by the use of power in subtly (or unabashedly) promoting personal and vested interests even when they conflict with organizational interests. Self-centered leaders are obsessed with power as a measure for dominating, controlling, and subjecting subordinates to their whims, caprices, and subjective views in order to eliminate perceived threats to their ideas, leadership style, positional relevance, and vested interests. They adopt an individualistic decision-making approach in order to prevent delegating authority to others so that they can execute their hidden agenda and self-centered schemes when opportunities arise. They are susceptible to the tendency of misusing and circumventing organizational regulations and usually resort to skewed improvisions and backdoor channels when resolving sensitive problems because this helps them keep a handle on their inordinate interests. The self-centered leader is one who personalizes work relationships, adopts an authoritarian management style, and deviates from the collectively adopted organizational practices in order to achieve self-focused goals (Hawass, 2018).

Evidence of self-serving behavior is more pronounced in the increasingly blatant manner in which organizational leaders distribute their organization's scarce resources. This could come in the form of perks and bonus increases, allocation of office space, and the use of equipment and other infrastructural tools. It could also come in the form of the prioritization and allotment of company funds to units and even in the way recognition is awarded. Due to the limited nature of resources, the more resources are allocated to one person, the less another or others can have from what is left. This leads to a form of power play in which the extent of power controlled by the leader acts as a predictor to influences that shape other self-serving leadership behaviors (Rus, Knippenberg, Wisse, 2010). Power is a noted factor with wide-ranging psychological and behavioral effects on how leaders perceive themselves, others, and their environment. These effects also differ depending on the level of hierarchical power that an individual enjoys since within an organization; there are leaders who enjoy more power than others.

The observation in this sense is that high-power leaders compared to low-power leaders, seem to show more behavioral sensitivity to their internal states and less sensitivity to information coming from the situational context (Rus, Knippenberg, Wisse, 2010). This means that the more powerful leader is more inclined to be controlled from the inside and has a tendency to pay more attention to personal preferences, feelings, idiosyncrasies, and beliefs. This makes them act more at will, exhibit a more goal-oriented disposition, care less about how others perceive their actions, and act in more variable ways with lesser susceptibility to the emotional demands of others. This could also be extended to showing lesser sensitivity and attention to social norms, the ideas and observations of others, relevant contextual information, and people's behavioral responses. In contradistinction, low power leaders seem to pay more attention to contextual cues than to their internal states and are thus more likely to be influenced by information derived from their environment than they are driven by their internal drives. They take in performance information, the normative culture in the organization, and the current contextual information as vital elements for processing their decisions and modulating their behavior. The implication of high-power leaders relying more on their internal states and not paying necessary attention to external cues is that it increases the risk of oversimplified assessments, stereotypic perceptions, and abuse of privilege over their subordinates. It also spikes the chances of self-serving, hidden, and aggressive behavior.

This influence of power on the functional approach of leaders (i.e., the pander to either internal or external sources of information) plays a significant role in shaping their self-centered behavior. The greater the power, the tendency for more resort to the personal filters that leaders engage internally. To the extent that their internal states are prejudiced by individual traits such as greed, insecurity, incompetence, ideological beliefs, or enhanced by more positive traits like a strong sense of focus, objectivity, motivation, and sound ethics, is the same extent to which they exhibit or curb self-serving traits. Understanding the role that power plays in shaping the psyche and behaviors of leaders is a good lever for developing mechanisms and evaluative assessments that can help the organization reduce the tendencies of leadership abuse. Low power leaders also have beliefs and are disposed to making references to them; nevertheless, the point is that they are more prone to considering external and organizational factors than their own stream of beliefs. This means they are more sensitive to their environment, use current information, and tend to abide by organizational practices; but it may also mean that they could be impressionable, easily unsettled, or compromise on their personal values. Nevertheless, high-power leaders who have self-centered beliefs and idiosyncrasies are more disposed to carrying out self-serving allocations, manipulations, and abuses.

The "I" Factor in Self-centered Leadership

From the foregoing, it is clear that mediocre leaders who display an excessive cling to individualistic proclivities and perspectives are often more aligned to a leadership ideology that strictly positions leadership opportunities only as a means to an end—the end, in this case, being the long-held aspirations, ambitions, and fantasies of these leaders. The internal configuration of their beliefs, value system, and convictions are slanted towards a competitive obsession that closely and progressively associates their self-image, self-worth, and self-actualization to positional and titular power. They become the center of their world, with everything bearing only relative importance or significance to them in respect to the achievement of their personal goals and ambitions. Such leaders, while rising through the ranks, only perceive TEAM and group membership as a necessary tool for ascending to their desired heights. While it is important that people are self-motivated and have clear life and career goals that they take relevant action to actualize, the difference with self-focused individuals is that people, positions, and organizations are seen primarily as objects. They do not become part of a system, society, community, organization, or group; instead, the group, organization, community, or system is seen as a part of their plan—they use people.

Some of them have been bold enough to argue that we all use people, systems, and things to reach our aspirations (i.e., achieve our "selfish" goals), and as a result, they argue that we are all selfish. However, the irony of the situation is that we are all likely to need people on our journey to becoming whatever we want to become—whether as selfish people or not. Nonetheless, the difference with selfish leaders is that apart from their microscopic personal goals, nothing else matters, or nothing else is considered of a significantly worthy value compared to their ambitions. They find themselves so blinded by their narrow thinking that they engage in myopic manipulations and activities that sometimes capsize the very boat that should take them to their destinations, or they destroy the supporting structures that should otherwise have preserved the possibility of attaining their aspirations. Their sense of judgment, perspective to issues, and interpretation of happenings are often constricted to the path that their self-centered thinking can afford them—though some are better able to exercise their faculties on a broader level than others. Generally, they are not able to develop broad-based innovative thinking that could help them provide excellent and outstanding leadership. This self-centered nature limits them to second-rate thinking, mediocre approaches, and mediocre results. They only become energetic about excellence when their positions are threatened or if they are in a competitive bid to assert themselves.

These leaders are more conscious and talk more about themselves than they talk about the TEAM. They are more "I" conscious than "we" conscious; thus, their language and actions reflect their isolation as independent entities from the group. They are quick to protect their interests regardless of what's best for the TEAM; they find it difficult to make sacrifices and are only motivated to get involved in any task when there is something in it for them. Self-centered leaders do only the least necessary to get their paycheck or fulfill their obligations and are quick to withdraw when things get tough. In leadership, they multiply avenues to "get all they can, and can all they get" and to perpetuate themselves in the most powerful positions for as long as they can, using every means at their disposal, whether legitimate or not.

Hawass (2019), in a recent study, proposed that self-centered leadership (SCL) traits can be captured under three primary constructs: i.e., personalism, individualism, and pseudo-institutionalism.

A. **Personalism:** This is when leaders view their relationships with others with a subjective and egocentric bias. Under this form of self-centered leadership, leaders deal with the organization as if it is their personal property and achieve their personal goals by using their positions to carry out self-interested activities that harm their subordinates and the organization. Under personalism, dominance motivation pushes the mediocre and self-centered leader to untoward acts that prioritize their self-propagation at the expense of their subordinates. Such leaders are bent on exercising control and bending the will of others and are not welcoming to talented, skilled, or promising subordinates. The quest for dominance and the attributes of insecurity become more pronounced when the social structure of the organization is unstable, especially when there is the likelihood of sudden institutional changes. Self-centered and mediocre leaders who exhibit personalism and its domination tendencies are less tolerant and considerate of others and show low social sensitivity to others (Nicol, 2009).

B. **Individualism:** This is used in a more specific sense, different from the generic sense in which it was initially used in the opening of this chapter. Individualism in this context refers to the tendency of a leader to make decisions regardless of the opinions submitted by other members of the group or TEAM; such that though other opinions or ideas are offered, such participative engagements are not appreciated in the decision-making process (Khadra, 1990; Hammad and Norris, 2009). This comes from a leadership disposition that emphasizes the need to assert the place of the leader as the one in charge and the chief determiner of the path the organization must follow. Hawass (2019), whose study focused on trends in Arab organizations, noted, for instance, that the Egyptian managers surveyed were often careful to ensure that the image of the big boss wasn't in any way undermined before subordinates, nor was organizational discipline sacrificed. As a result, it was largely perceived that the way to preserve the leader's image and to ensure employee discipline was that deliberations and suggestions were made only in a way that showed that the decision would be made at the top. Under individualism, it is believed that for leaders to be respected, they need to be distant and tough; thus, authoritarianism and non-participation by the rank and file in decision-making are seen as prerequisites to sustaining reverence and discipline.

Personalism and individualism are complementary to each other because the subjectivism and egocentrism of personalism are reinforced by the authoritarian and non-participatory blend of individualism. Leaders in such mold, in order to resolve work-related problems or difficulties, often have to employ informal arrangements and sometimes manipulate formal structures. They create a system of double standards, one in which they selectively use organizational regulations to legitimize their practices, and in other instances, adopt behind-the-curtain approaches to handle persistent corporate challenges (Hawass, 2019).

C. **Pseudo-institutionalism:** This is a situation in which managers and leaders are significantly confined to certain strict organizational systems, procedures, and rules, such that they cannot avoid them. This is because the organization may have independent controlling entities or some other measures by which they keep a close tab on institutional compliance. However, what these leaders and managers do is to accept the company's procedures, laid-down rules, and system in theory but to alter it in practice. For instance, they could ensure surface compliance with the required formalities for documentation but find loopholes in the rules that help them tailor the regulations in such a way that it fulfills their personal objectives. Their commitment to corporate, organizational, or institutional processes is superficial because at the back of it is an ingrained quest and attendant smartness to exploit the rules to their advantage. Pseudo-institutionalism also correlates with personalism and individualism, and together they buttress the fundamental elements through which self-centered leadership finds expression.

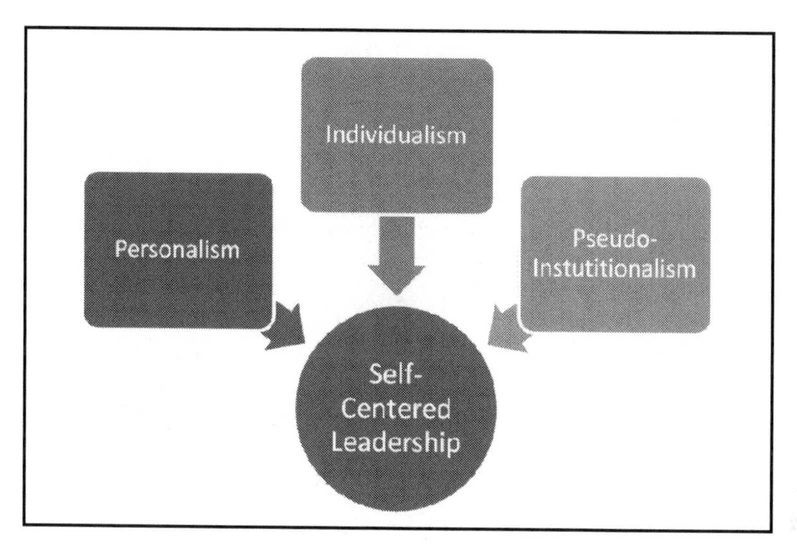

Fig 8.1 Three Major Traits of Self-Centered Leadership (SCL)

The Demerits of Self-Centered Leadership

One of the cardinal demerits of self-centered leadership is that apart from undermining the organization and putting it at grave risk, it could weaken the TEAM, slow down innovation and create a toxic culture in the organization. Self-centered leadership is a direct attack and affront on group and TEAM orientations. It essentially undermines those great attributes that great TEAMs are known for, especially when they operate in stiffly competitive and rapidly changing environments. Listed below are some of the demerits.

1. It creates a toxic culture of greed, selfishness, and unhealthy rivalry. The organization becomes a means to an end, and its interests are not protected.

2. It weakens TEAM/group leverage and comparative advantage. Leverage in the most apposite context of the word here simply refers to the use of the areas of comparative advantage, advantageous factors, qualities, tools, or networks in order to achieve certain goals

without a commensurate expenditure of financial resources. It is using all advantages that a company has to maintain a competitive edge without necessarily spending as much. When leaders dominate their TEAM members and do not allow them to contribute their quota because of individualism, they lose out on vital competencies, skills, talents, and other aspects of human resources that could have helped the organization.

3. There is no synergy. A leader determines what ways or patterns employees and subordinates will follow. If leaders show a self-centered approach to work, their subordinates are likely to follow in the same steps, and this will reduce the level of cooperation that would exist within the firm. This would also lead to unease and increased interpersonal tensions between employees competing to corner opportunities for individual gain. Energy will be lost and dissipated along the work chains, and the systems wouldn't function at their best. It is simply not a TEAM at work but separate entities groveling for disparate personal interests.

4. Mediocrity triumphs over excellence. Self-centered leaders aren't willing to allow others to outshine them and will likely not tolerate talent and competence. Two common ways way they usually do this is to ensure they don't hire talented employees or to bog them down with mundane job roles that will deny them the opportunity for recognition.

5. Lack of transparency and accountability. The manipulative tendencies of self-centered leaders also make their subordinates with similar ambitions learn the ropes of opaqueness, hypocrisy, and how to cut corners. This will weaken accountability and obfuscate otherwise simple processes with needless complexities.

6. Employees lose their sense of belonging. This happens more when employees or subordinates are not recognized for their hard work and contributions and are always made to take the back seat during recognition, despite the immense value they bring to the table. This leads to dissatisfaction, and aggrieved employees begin to feel alienated from the company. They will also begin to seek opportunities elsewhere or square up for dirty office politics—i.e., for those incensed to get a piece of the pie, come what may. In any case, none of such scenarios is good for a company or organization that has a future.

7. Ideation and innovation die. When a company has no ventilation system through which new ideas come in, it naturally begins to lose out on the innovation front. Leaders who have dominated the top for long and whose ideas have been the sole source of direction and inspiration will soon begin to wear out, and so will their ideas and the innovative capacities of the organization. It is crucial that organizations checkmate the self-centered tendencies of their leaders and create either internal or external support networks that help to inject fresh ideas and innovation into the organization. This is an indispensable factor required to sustain vibrancy and growth.

8. Mental fatigue and burn-out. When self-centered leaders overwhelm themselves with cumbersome responsibilities and tasks in order to feel on top of their units, organizations, or subordinates, they could eventually burn themselves out and induce mental fatigue. Oftentimes, this happens when these leaders haven't attained the heights they desire and still have thirsts and longings that haven't been satisfied; otherwise, the usual situation is that such leaders only do the necessary to keep their positions of influence and to service their interests. Mental fatigue is the result of overburdening

> their faculties with mundane processes and subordinate activities whilst still engaging in the demands of upper management responsibilities.

As has already been noted and discussed throughout this book, leadership is essentially about mobilizing people towards the achievement of visionary goals and objectives. However, where the followers sense their objectification by the leader and that there are no real ideals, visionary commitments, and futuristic plans that cater for the organization in the long term and by implication the future of their careers, they will also develop an adaptive isomorphism which could take on different forms. Self-centered leadership relies heavily on the use of power, domination, and manipulation of existing systems. This means that apart from scrutinizing the individual and leadership orientations of leaders, it is important that organizations create effective checks and balances, promote an open corporate culture, and ensure effective communication channels to keep the organization healthy. This way, they will significantly shield their internal systems from circumvention and reduce the selfish, dominating, and devastating impacts of self-centered leaders.

CHAPTER NINE

REMORSELESS NATURE
LACK OF SYMPATHY AND UNCARING

"Most people have no imagination. If they could imagine the sufferings of others, they would not make them suffer so."
— Anna Funder

Case Study: Panera Bread

In this story, Brandon Cook, a 21-year-old student, regularly visited his grandmother, who was dying of cancer, in the hospital. She craved soup but hated the hospital food. She instead preferred clam chowder from Panera. However, Panera only sold clam chowder on Fridays, and on this particular day, Brandon's grandmother wanted clam chowder; it was not Friday.

Brandon loved his grandmother and knew she did not have much time to live. Watching her die slowly was challenging every day. He wanted to make her happy as much as he could. Brandon had probably not eaten his grandmother's hospital food, but he could imagine how bad it was, and he felt she deserved better. He didn't want to wait to get his grandmother what she craved because he was unsure how long she had to live.

Brandon called up the local Panera, contacting the manager. He explains the situation to the manager, who is touched by Brandon's love for his grandma. She understands what it feels like to know you are about to lose someone who means so much to you and trying to make them happy as much as you can. So even though it wasn't Friday, the manager decides to go out of her way to make the clam chowder. She tells Brandon when he can come pick it up.

When Brandon got to the Panera in Nashua, New Hampshire, the manager gave him the clam chowder and a box of cookies. The manager did not know Brandon's grandmother and didn't know if she liked cookies, but she was aware of how most people feel about cookies and believed that a free box of cookies would likely make Brandon's grandmother happier.

Brandon was greatly moved by the kindness of the Panera manager to him and his family. He decided to repay the favor. He wanted others to know what transpired so that they could know how kindness still exists in the world. Brandon posted the Panera story on his Facebook wall for his friends to see. For him, it was the best way to tell the story to as many of his friends as possible.

Interestingly, Brandon's mother, Gail Cook, saw his wall post. She admired her son's initiative and care for his grandmother. She was also impressed by the kindness and generosity of the manager at her local Panera. She then reposts Brandon's wall post onto Panera Bread's fan page. Soon, the story circulated like wildfire. In less than two weeks, Brandon's post had been liked almost 750,000 times and had received nearly 32,000 comments. The kindness and caring nature of the manager of Panera helped to promote her brand in a new way with greater possibilities.

There are many leaders who are uncomfortable with this topic because of what they perceive to be its underlying meaning and implication. One of the trails in mediocre thinking that often accompany a discourse on the subject of remorse and empathy is that it is considered inappropriate in a corporate setting. It is believed to interfere with the rationality of the decision-making process and is viewed as a sign of weakness. The reasons for these misconceptions stem from the fact that many of these leaders themselves lack empathy; they think empathy is fleeting and see it as an effeminate notion of "pity" (Holt & Marques, 2012). They dissociate business success from such an emotional element and the attendant components of the soft side of human nature involved. Unfortunately, studies show that there is an increasing need to incorporate the teaching of this and other critical "soft skills" in the training of business leaders and students because research shows their low appreciation for its value (Brown, Sautter, Littvay, Sautter, & Bearnes, 2010).

Remorse within the scope of the discussion in this chapter actually relates to the virtue of empathy, and this goes a little beyond the situational exhibition of sympathy (i.e., the virtue of showing compassion and sensitivity to others in distress). This is because empathy is the innate virtue and ability to experience and relate to the thoughts, emotions, or experiences of others on a consistent basis. Empathy tries to feel and see as the other person, while sympathy may not exactly feel what the person feels, but identifies with the person and shows compassion. Empathy is another fundamental component of leadership recognized by various leadership theories, and it plays a fundamental role in helping leaders and managers in crisis management (Gentry, Weber, & Sadri, 2016; König, Graf-Vlachy, Bundy & Little, 2018).

In the area of boss-to-subordinate relations in the workplace, one of the most significant questions that psychologists have asked and have attempted to answer is whether power causes leaders to develop insensitivity to others and whether it makes them incapable of empathy. Interestingly, findings have pointed to links between occupying positions of power and a reduced ability in visualizing, interpreting, or understanding the cognitive, emotional, or perceptive disposition of others (Inzlicht & Obhi, 2014). In comparison, those who occupy lesser positions of power or social status seem to show a better aptitude for the visual, cognitive, and emotional communication and postures of other people. Psychologists tell us that the human brain, through what is known as the mirror system, has the ability to be especially attuned to other people. This system is made up of a network of regions in the brain that becomes active when you perform an action and are also closely involved when you are observing another person performing the same action (Inzlicht & Obhi, 2014). It is this process that helps us to resonate with the actions of others, understand what they are doing, and somewhat share in the experience. However, this ability seems to show a reduced effect depending on the level of positional power that those evaluated possess.

Some experts have noted that the underlying reason for the empathy distance between leaders and their subordinates is traceable to a couple of factors, one of which is that powerful people are often in a position where they have plentiful access to important resources, and so they do not seem dependent on people below them to get the vital access they need. When necessary, they are able to deploy resources from their sophisticated network to meet their needs, and this gives them a greater sense of sufficiency, making people more dispensable to them. If they can't get what they want from you, they will get it from someone or somewhere else. Another position that has emerged on this point is the observation that when people experience power, there is an accompanying change in their brains that impacts how sensitive they are to the actions of others (Inzlicht & Obhi, 2014). This, however, doesn't mean that the powerful are incapable of empathy or sympathy since power in itself isn't always an inherently resident factor but one that is usually acquired.

These neurological changes only imply a lower motivation to care by those with greater power, but this low motivation could be altered by possessing a progressive set of orientations, perspectives, and cognition that emphasize the skill and value of understanding people and connecting with them. Some studies have linked the development of empathy as a sign of improved brain maturity (Holt & Marques, 2012). This is an indication that even though the acquisition of power tends to neurologically reduce the empathy level of leaders, those with well-developed and mature brain activity on the job will better appreciate the value of empathy and apply themselves to it since it can be learned. More so, the fact that it can be learned means it can also be taught. This training in empathy development is pivotal to developing the relevant maturity leaders need to deploy in people and organizational management. In a study carried out some years ago, business students, especially those in finance, who lacked empathy, were observed to be narcissists. They showed a tendency to cheat, were less cooperative, and more likely to defect in bargaining games (Brown et al., 2010). Interestingly, it is these traits that follow them into their careers, causing them to exhibit antisocial tendencies like being manipulative, being self-centered, and in extreme cases, becoming psychopathic.

Unsympathetic Leadership

Excellent leaders keep their eyes on the goal, but they also do not lose sight of the needs of their TEAM members. They play hard on the field but know how to sympathize with a member of the TEAM when necessary. Sympathy is the act of showing compassion and sensitivity to others in distress. Being sympathetic here involves being moved with compassion about a person's suffering or distress to the point of taking action to relieve the person of the distress. Rinpoche (1992) defines compassion as:

"...not simply a sense of sympathy or caring for the person suffering, not simply a warmth of heart toward the person before you, or a sharp recognition of their needs and pain, it is also a sustained and practical determination to do whatever is possible and necessary to help alleviate their suffering."

Analysts and commentators have severally made a case for more compassion in the workplace, raising concerns in several articles about the current dearth of sympathy in corporate life (Poorkavoos, 2016). This is despite the huge amount of literature in the last two decades that has emerged on the subject of emotional intelligence and the attendant popularity that the discussion has enjoyed both within the corporate and academic environments. One would have thought that with such fanciful seminars, conferences, and literature, corporate executives would be more upbeat about showing sympathy and improving in their compassionate gestures. However, research within this period seems to point to the contrary (Bradberry & Greaves, 2005; Poorkavoos, 2016). The emotional intelligence quotient of many corporate leaders and managers seems to rise as they make their way up the ladder but soon plateaus at the managerial level and begins to diminish significantly as they climb higher through other positions, climaxing adversely at the position of CEO. This corroborates the earlier findings that depict a rise in position and power increases leaders' insensitivity to others. The irony of the situation, it seems, is that those who need emotional intelligence the most have it in short supply even with growing evidence that emotional intelligence is a better predictor of performance than just technical skill, intellect, or how long a person has served a company.

This means that many subordinates function on a stronger level of emotional intelligence than their superiors, especially those in the C-suite class or its equivalent. This contradiction further means that there is a greater tendency for subordinates to display better people skills than those who lead them. While this might not be a problem if the superior functions above average, it can portend a frustrating challenge for employees where the leader operates below par in basic people skills. Mediocre leaders who are devoid of empathy and who cannot show others sympathy in their times of distress will also find themselves unable to show attributions of compassion in times of corporate need or crisis (König, 2018). This makes it difficult to gain the attention and trust of affected stakeholders and investors in a crisis situation, in turn putting the leadership prospects of such unsympathetic leaders in question. Managing periods of crises require that leaders are able to identify in sympathetic terms with the stakeholders affected and to be able to communicate concern, sincere interest, and care. Such leaders are also in a better position to be trusted to objectively protect the interests of those involved, properly diagnose problematic areas, and make more relevant prognostications on possible solutions.

Unsympathetic leaders are simply ill-equipped to handle certain forms of crises, especially the people side of things. The effective attribution of compassion is a vital component to providing what experts identify as instructing and adjusting information in times of crisis (Coombs, 2015). Instructing information consists of all relevant information and communication that helps those affected by a crisis situation to avoid immediate harm and to also identify immediate lines of action that need to be taken. Adjusting information involves all relevant information and communication that helps stakeholders manage the psychological and emotional impacts of the crisis. Leaders who have not developed the ability to be sympathetic or to show empathy will find themselves alienated from the right language, insights, and disposition that they need to exhibit, especially to stakeholders and also to the employees they need to uplift and inspire to action at such critical times. Mediocre leaders, through their unsympathetic behavior, create a hostile environment in which solidarity between co-workers is strained. This makes commitment more mechanical than affective, while line supervisors, managers, and unit heads will lack the enthusiasm needed to provide close support for the people they have oversight of. This is because the air is generally individualistic, excessively formalistic, and leaves little or no room for co-workers to share a common sense of belonging, comradeship, or a bond of affinity. When leaders lack sympathy, their attitude can negatively impact the culture of the organization.

Compassion breeds compassion, and this reciprocal cycle light up the firm like a chain reaction, strengthening interpersonal and intra-organizational relationships. When employees know that their bosses care about their wellbeing, especially when they need it the most, it increases their job satisfaction, and this helps to strengthen employee retention. Employees will, in turn, likely show deeper levels of commitment, loyalty, and support, especially at crucial periods when the organization needs such goodwill from its staff. A 2013 study is reported to have corroborated the effect of compassionate leadership in reducing employee turnover. Employee turnover in an organization was reduced by 60% after a new initiative encouraged employees to express compassion to each other regularly (Poorkavoos, 2016: pg. 10). Mediocre and unsympathetic leaders cannot appreciate the significance of retaining a talented workforce and securing employee loyalty, they have a posture like they can always get what they want, and this is true until they lose some of their finest hands. They are more likely to think every problem can be solved by money. They change people often or source for the skill they need outside the organization. Their time of reckoning comes during difficult times when there is a limit to the expendable resources available. They often fare badly, are unable to resourcefully save money, and cannot inspire their TEAM to action through shared ideals.

Two Streams of Leadership Care

Reference at this point will be made to Heidegger's complex organizational concept of solicitude (called Fürsorge), which has been interpreted in more contemporary language as care (Tomkins & Simpson, 2015). The difference that the Heideggerian concept brings to the table is that it makes far-reaching contentions and postulations on the concept of care as engagement within the organization rather than just an act of sympathy that is carried out only when there is distress. Here, care is closely associated with the everyday activity of the organization as an in-the-world sense of activity, in which engagement, connection, and concern must bear an intrinsic expression in what goes on in the life of the organization. This in-the-world sense of engagement, connection, and concern in the organization's life is the relational sense in which the individual is seen as an integral part of the organization. It is also in this sense that the leader is examined on how he engages with this world—i.e., whether he shows concern for the things in that world (called Besorgen) or whether he shows care for the people in that world (called Fürsorge). Essentially, Heidegger's first contention is that care is about engagement, connection, and concern in an everyday sense, touching on practical dealings with projects and systems (i.e., things) and then with people in the organization.

In this sense, the uncaring attitude and disposition of a leader is captured intrinsically as disengagement, disconnection, and "dis-concern" with the world they were actually contracted to interact with, particularly in relation to the people in that world—though it is doubtful that this won't extend to the realm of the things of the organization. For these leaders, even though they oversee activities, drive the TEAM to achieve goals, and occupy positional roles in strategy and decision-making, their detachment from this world puts a limit on the quality of service they can offer. They are also likely to be more conscious of their hierarchical position, which further makes them use power distance to stay aloof from TEAM engagement. It is, of course, common knowledge that hierarchical leadership has its good uses as we have in the military, paramilitary, and other forms of organizations, but companies that want to be competitive, innovative, and creative need transformational and transactional leaders who can sustain a robust connection and engagement with the TEAM. It is these leaders that can build a culture of reciprocal solidarity, forge synergy, and unleash the innovative potentials inherent in TEAMwork. It is also trite knowledge that history has shown that some of the most outstanding military leaders we have seen were transactional and transformational in their build.

With further expatiation on the concept of care in leadership, Heidegger identifies two streams of interventions through which care flows in an organization, i.e.

- ***The Care of Substitutive Intervention,*** in which the leader "leaps in" to put himself in the other person's place due to a particular situation, problem, or distress for as long as it takes for it to abate. In this scenario, the leader takes responsibility to direct the resolution of the problem or distress, and once it is resolved, disengages from the situation—in other instances, there could be a re-engagement of sorts in the original roles or other alterations as deemed fit.

- ***The Care of Suggestive Intervention,*** in which the leader 'leaps ahead' to point out possibilities, potentials, and options through which the recipient of the care can solve the problem or distress at hand. This form of care is a suggestive, enabling, and facilitative model of intervention that isn't exactly geared towards spearheading a particular course of action but is more attuned to opening up possible options for adoption by the care recipient (Tomkins & Simpson, 2015).

These two approaches of ***leaping-in*** and ***leaping-ahead*** are delineated to respectively focus on the immediate and on the future. Leaping-in tackles immediate challenges and, in a way, correlates with a form of transactional engagement, while leaping-ahead reaches beyond the immediate with a futuristic approach and correlates with a form of transformational engagement. This means that caring leaders who are able to effectively jump in on situations to provide a form of care to those who need it are exercising themselves effectively in transactional leadership, while those who exercise the suggestive and enabling form of leadership care are being transformational at that moment. In relating to the present and future, leaders should embrace the function of temporality.

Temporality involves the deliberate attempt to contextualize immediate interventions with useful knowledge from the past and thoroughly assessed cues from projections on the likely future in order to sort out present challenges. It also involves handling leaping-ahead with a good and thorough grasp of the past and assessment of the present in order to shape and choose the future. For leaping-in, the relevant knowledge gained from past and future assessments are done in order to emphasize grounding the immediate care in what is definite and certain. While in the area of leaping ahead, the emphasis of knowing is on the intimation of the past and present in order to identify credible options and possibilities for the future.

These two approaches help enhance leaping-in in the immediate with the virtue of openness to futuristic thinking while enhancing leaping-ahead and futuristic options with the clarity and focus that come from a sound background analysis. Leaders who show care must ensure that their attempts aren't done in a way that humiliates or belittles the recipient and that they do not get to a point where the quest for certainty in providing care blinds them to possible uncertainties and the influence of the past. They should also not allow thoughts of the future to overshadow the need to take cues from the present—when in fact, the present is what actually exists. Whichever way, the uncaring leader who lacks these transactional and transformational qualities will be too simplistic and quite stodgy. These qualities have been associated with leadership care under the present discourse, but it all actually begins with the leader's initiative to connect with his TEAM in order to maximize the potentials of the TEAM and sustain the individual resourcefulness of TEAM members.

Remorse and Sympathy can be Learned

Leaders who are desirous of leading change in their organizations need remorse to show their subordinates and followers that their contributions are valued, and their interests are important. This also helps leaders to become aware of the people in their world who make things happen, which is why researchers are increasingly emphatic about emotional and social intelligence. Findings show that empathy is positively related to job performance, and countries with high levels of power distance have shown a record of managers who show empathy performing better (Gentry, Weber, & Sadri, 2016). This is despite the fact that countries with high levels of power-distance emphasize hierarchy and formalities; however, these findings show that in these countries, empathy increases the opportunities and potentials of managers to perform. The paternalistic nature of cultures with high power-distance in which leaders have a paternal disposition and feel obligated to protect their subordinates is what makes empathy have a high correlation for successful leadership in these cultures. Leaders today need to be more person-focused in order to be successful with leading cross-cultural, cross-departmental, and cross-organizational TEAMs. They will also find themselves having to interact and deal with diverse social groups, people with different histories, perspectives, and idiosyncrasies. Such contemporary demands on leadership make empathy crucial to leadership success in today's complex environments.

In addition to the factors already mentioned above that influence the development of empathy, the Institute of Cognitive Neuroscience of the University College London (UCL) has noted in a study that young people show a lesser capability in exhibiting empathy and empathy-based emotions than those more advanced in age. The study based its findings on an analysis of the role of the medial prefrontal cortex of the brain in high-level thinking, empathy, guilt, and the interpretation of other people's motivations. The study found that in teenagers, this part of the brain was underutilized in their decision-making process and that maturity brings about a development of the brain that shifts activities more from the back to the front, thus facilitating a more robust development of essential soft skills through this prefrontal cortex area. However, empathy-based behaviors can be learned and inculcated in a way that the emotions of others can be perceived and interpreted. One tool that can be used is learning to ask questions that facilitate interpersonal understanding, build connections between people, and help interpret the emotional state of people (Weinstein, 2009).

Another important tool is to identify and clarify the core values and beliefs that one has and to see what correlation exists between those beliefs and their impact on the day-to-day interactions within the organization (Eriksen, 2009). Leadership and management development programs that train leaders in these skills are also a good avenue for helping leaders develop along this line (Mahsudet al., 2010). Classroom teaching has been considered as another good platform for imparting these traits (Izenberg, 2007). This is useful especially for teenagers and those taking professional tertiary courses. Although, some experts have argued that such teaching is preferably called "therapy" and should be taught by those specially certified in this area. In addition to the avenues and platforms mentioned, another platform that has been identified for learning such skills is through the teachings and practices of religious and spiritual discipline (Devay, 2010).

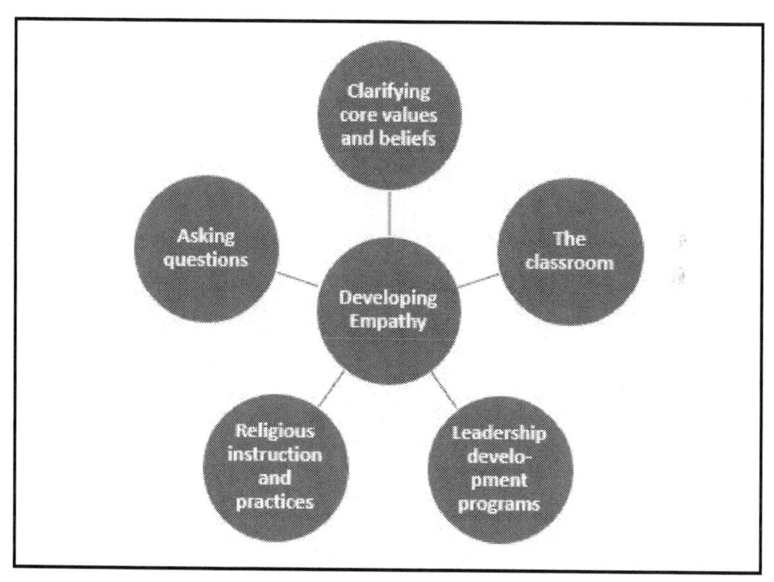

Fig 9.1 Steps and Avenues for Learning Empathy

Leaders who want to increase their capacities to show compassion and care and who want to elevate the level of solidarity and compassion exchange in their organization can do so by asking the following questions and undertaking the accompanying measures identified in the box below.

Table 9.1 Model questions and measures to help leaders foster a culture of compassion in their organizations:

1. Do I actively promote a culture of mutual respect, trust, and openness, in which co-workers and TEAM members know that talking about their problems or difficulties openly will not earn them censure, condemnation, or scorn from the leadership or other TEAM members, but instead people will listen and try to help?

2. As a leader, does my disposition show I care about my people and that I show concern in their difficult moments?

3. Do I actively encourage members of the TEAM to lend a helping hand to fellow colleagues who are in distress or difficult situations?

4. What is my belief about sharing problems with others? Do I consider it to be a worthy value?

5. How often and through what measures can I promote contact and interaction among members of staff within my organization?

6. Can I gauge the level of connection between members of my TEAM? Do members of staff feel heard, seen, and known, instead of being in the shadows?

7. What is the degree of openness in the organization? And to what extent do fellow colleagues feel free to approach each other if they notice a person has a problem?

8. How do I normalize a culture of checking on each other just to be sure the other person is doing fine?

9. Is there confidentiality and a sense of solidarity that makes fellow colleagues respect each other's privacy and feelings? Is there a culture not to violate the trust and confidentiality reposed?

10. To what extent do people feel free to openly express their emotional pain or to mention a certain difficulty they are dealing with?

CHAPTER TEN

MEDIOCRE LEADERSHIP AND TEAM CULTURE – TACKLING SECOND-RATE LEADERSHIP AND MEDIOCRE TEAM CULTURE

"We try to have the kind of a culture that doesn't value excuses in the sense that when you're supposed to accomplish something, and you're at a high level, then your job is to accomplish it, in spite of difficulty. And you're rewarded for dealing with that."
– Phil Libin

Case Study: Zappos

A marketplace for shoes isn't most likely the only thing that comes to mind when the name Zappos pops up. While the company is an online marketplace for shoes and other retail goods, it is not what Zappos sells that makes it stand out. It is how it sells (more precisely, what it does for its employees and customers) that makes Zappos what it is today. The company makes over $1 billion in revenue annually. In 2009 Amazon acquired Zappos for around $1 billion. The acquisition by Amazon was not the typical transaction where the founder and the TEAM get rich and retire from the company. Till today Zappos still operates independently from Amazon. A quick look at the Zappos website might make anyone think it is a competitor of Amazon.

Zappos has become almost as famous for its culture as it is for its shoes online. Their company culture begins with a cultural fit interview, which to a large extent determines whether the candidate will be hired or not. New employees are said to be offered $2,000 to quit after the first week of training if they believe the job is not okay for them. Employee raises come from passing skill tests and exhibiting increased capability and not from office politics. The company's budget is designed to cover employee TEAM building and culture promotion.

In addition, ten core values are instilled in every TEAM member. The company defined its corporate culture with these core values. The HR and management TEAM develops employee job descriptions, outlines the hiring process, and ensures regular on-the-job training. The day-to-day work environment reminds and reinforces the following core values with employees, visitors, customers, and partners:

- Deliver WOW Through Service
- Embrace and Drive Change
- Create Fun and A Little Weirdness
- Be Adventurous, Creative, and Open-Minded
- Pursue Growth and Learning
- Build Open and Honest Relationships through Communication
- Build a Positive Team and Family Spirit
- Do More with Less
- Be Passionate and Determined
- Be Humble

Besides being distinctive, these cardinal values create a framework for Zappos' actions. These values guide everything they do, including how they interact with their employees, how they interact with their customers and community, and how they interact with their vendors and business partners.

As stated earlier, Zappos hires according to cultural fit. Having established what the company culture is, fitting into that culture is an essential criterion that they consider when hiring. This further promotes and reinforces the company culture, which leads to happy employees, and eventually leads to happy customers. Zappos takes certain specific actions daily that reinforce its culture of being a fun workplace.

Just like Zappos, you need to create a work environment that provides employees with a sense of belonging, meaningful work, and incentives and do away with monotony, lack of openness, and mediocre thinking.

Great benefits and a fun workplace dedicated to making customers happy fits right in with Zappos' approach to company culture. When you get the company culture right, excellent customer service and an exceptional brand become more feasible.

The only way to tackle mediocrity is to place a premium on outstanding performance and to entrench in the value system of the organization a culture of excellence. In reality, while organizations that desire enduring excellence look beyond immediate short-term goals and set their focus towards sustaining long-term competitive advantage(s) and business success strategies, it is also true that even in the short term, they do not want mediocre results. Business success is a cumulative process; therefore, the day-to-day and short-term goals of an organization ought to be part of its big picture and should have a bearing on its long-term goals, objectives, and vision. Engendering a culture of excellence and rooting out mediocrity requires that organizations find the most effective, efficient, and innovative ways to carry out their activities and fulfill their vision and mission. Excellence is a state of affairs, thinking, and commitment that prioritizes and emphasizes the best ethics, ideas, methods, tools, and finesse in carrying out the activities of the organization. Excellence can, therefore, be described as a way of being, thinking, and a commitment to activate operational modus that reaches beyond mediocrity (Suciu, 2017).

Mediocrity, on the other hand, involves only a modest commitment to the highest quality of thoughts, ideas, methods, tools, and ethics. It is a mid-level range of commitment that omits higher levels of values, practices, and ideas but which also projects a commitment that cannot be relegated as abysmal or poor. Such leaders or employees only show occasional, conditional, or modest interests in adopting best practices, rigorous processes, and innovative thinking in the course of their responsibilities. They only do what is enough to achieve some kind of positive result or fulfill their duties. These leaders don't go the extra mile, and their level of commitment is not as good as it could be, neither is it as bad as it could get, rather it is mediocre (Berman and West, 2003). Therefore, creating a culture of excellence and providing excellent leadership will require that both leaders and their organizations have a proactive disposition towards creating the future by envisioning possibilities, identifying best practices, and putting in place organizational systems and corporate strategies that are forward-looking. Leaders and other members of the TEAM also need to work in concert to ensure the adoption of such qualitative inputs that will generate the excellent outcomes that they desire.

Leadership effectiveness requires a combination of different factors ranging from having the right traits, skills, behaviors, and methods to upholding the right values, building the right atmosphere and systems, and encouraging the right ideas. Studies show that leaders that exhibit some specific characteristics, prioritize learning, are goal-oriented, good at interpersonal communication, and are self-confident have a higher tendency to be effective leaders who can also bring about increased levels of organizational excellence and effectiveness (De Lacerda, 2015). Leaders play a critical role in how effective, productive, and supportive the culture within their organization becomes, while the organizational culture plays a role in shaping the future leadership of the firm through acculturation as people grow through the ranks. Acculturation is the process by which employees learn the ways of the organization over time and imbibe both the written rules and unspoken rules of the organization, leading to either positive or negative consequences depending on the nature of the existing internal culture—i.e., whether it is progressive or retrogressive, proactive or reactive, whether it is open and dynamic, or whether it is closed and rigid.

The Influence of Leadership on Team Culture

Apart from the negative influences that the personal deficiencies of leaders inflict on organizations—which we have already extensively adumbrated in each chapter of this book—there is a difference between leaders who are pioneers of groups and those who emerge as leaders from the group. This particular analysis has more to do with the impact of leadership style on the organization's culture as against the impact of the leader's individual deficiency. In the first case, leaders who are pioneers exact overwhelming influence on the formative and directional course of the organization and on its culture. In the second situation, emergent leaders do not create the culture of the organization; instead, they themselves emerge from the existing culture and are expected to have acquired the identity, values, and orientation of the organization. As a result, their promotion is usually based on an assessment of their cultural fit, competence, contributions, and the prospects of their leadership within the larger picture of the organization's current and future development.

This is the case if the existing culture is one that is considered progressive and has been instrumental to the success of the organization. However, where the culture is retrogressive, stale, or bland, a leader could be brought from outside the organization to bring about change; or one with the right build from within the company could be appointed with a mandate to lead the desired change. Pioneering leaders create new corporate cultures, while emergent leaders play a role in the maintenance, enhancement/ depreciation, and evolution of existing cultures.

When we talk of change, we are essentially referring to a shift in culture and also in business outcomes. In shifting the culture of the organization, the focus of the leader is on the people, and the concern is about attuning them to the required changes that will keep or make the organization more relevant in the market based on prevailing conditions. Unlike the first situation in which the pioneer leader is the creator of the culture that guides the organization in its formative years; in the second case, the leader inherits a system, and depending on how successful or problematic the inherited system is, the leader's role is essentially to enhance the existing culture or evolve a new culture. This process is arguably more engaging because the changes the new leader is trying to make will have to compete with the pre-existing culture, which at this point has become quite stable and entrenched. Change is usually a sensitive and difficult process that requires a good combination of leadership skills, communication effectiveness, and foresight. The first point being made here about the influence of leaders on an organization's culture is that founders of organizations have a predominant influence on the culture their organizations develop in their formative years up to any given time when they still have strong leadership control on the firm.

Leaders who emerged through the system are more likely to have acquired the key assumptions about the identity and values of the organization and are promoted based on their cultural fit and contribution within the organization (Schein, 2015). Although they could also become change agents who see the need to adapt the internal culture to the realities of the changing external environment; the second point being made here is that in determining what is expected of a leader, it is important to consider whether the leader is coming in at the formative stage of the organization, or whether the leader is new to the system and has been brought in to change its culture and business outcomes. The complexities involved lie in the fact that founding leaders will find the thought stream of new leaders to be significantly different, which could be what the organization needs.

There is also the challenge that leaders who have grown through the system may come under the effect of groupthink, but it might be more advantageous if an organization is lucky to find a leader from within with the right build to bring change. Truly, such a leader may have emerged from the system, but he is more likely to be able to suggest and manage more complex ideas and situations through his better aptitude of the organization. Taking the discourse from a situational theory perspective, leadership that is faced with creating or evolving the culture in an organization will have to adapt its engagement of employees in a manner that effectively uses the directive, consultative, supportive, and delegative forms of leadership engagement (Rosiński, 2017; Hersey, Blanchard & Johnson, 2015).

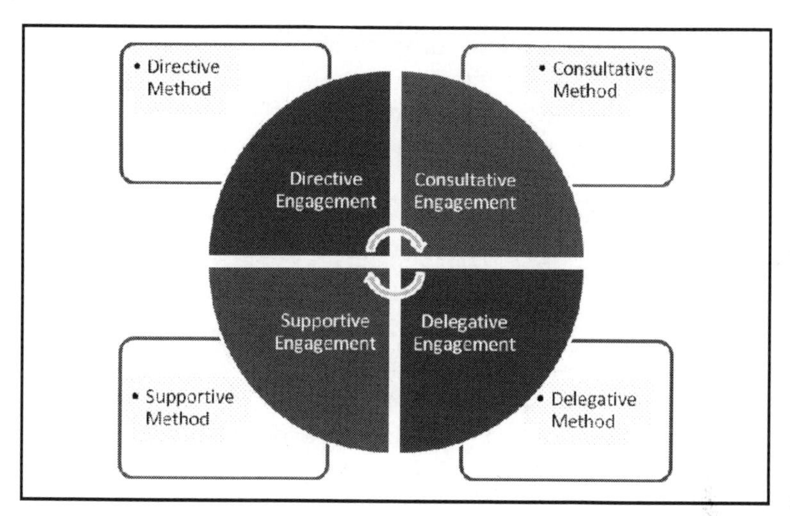

Fig 10.1 Four Ways to Engage Employees in Fulfilling Organizational Tasks

When leadership adopts a predominance of just one method, take, for instance, the directive method of engagement, its leadership results are bound to be poor because this singular form of engagement cannot be suited to all situations. Also, where it engages two of the methods, it will achieve an average and mediocre result. Engaging all four measures skillfully and appropriately is instrumental to helping employees develop the right response to work, while the leader is better able to create the right work environment. Delegation, for example, empowers subordinates, is a form of inclusion and makes employees learn faster.

However, if a leader is constantly delegating sensitive responsibilities to TEAM members at the formative or early stage where no clear mode of operation or organizational style is discernible to the employees in question, it could create accidents in the accomplishment of objectives as these employees do not yet have a firm grasp of how they are to act. As a result of their immature knowledge of the workings of the organization, or due to the fledgling nature of its style, these employees are bound to act based on their own ideas or judgment, which could increase the events of accidents. On the other hand, when an organization has advanced considerably in its style, and an employee is significantly clear on the operational mode, an excessive cling to directive leadership in which the leader scarcely delegates to employees will create dissatisfaction and discontent, especially among competent employees. This could also set a tone for tensions in the organization or lead to a loss of talented staff to organizations where they can grow and express their potentials.

Being consultative and supportive is a good way to engage the intelligence, originality, and participation of employees in decision-making. It also includes a form of coaching that allows employees to correct their mistakes, improve on their jobs, and have the leader pay attention to their personal needs. However, any excessive lean towards the personal concerns of employees can create situations in which employees become indulged, and their personal matters could become exaggerated in order to gain the leader's attention, negotiate compromises on delivery, or buy more time for the execution of tasks. This will, in turn, compromise the efficacy within the organization and create excuses, subpar results, and a culture of mediocre functionality.

There are several scenarios that show the need for leaders to be adept in their combination of engagement methods. Another instance is that leaders, who are inclined toward the consultative model, may engage it instead of the directive model when dealing with new employees who are still learning the ropes. This will cause a drag on the leader's time, while the quality of work done by the employee may have to be reviewed severally by the leader because it may be below expectation. At this stage of the employee or organizational development, a directive approach is better because instead of expending a lot of time guiding the employee to the desired end, the leader can at once tell the employee what is expected and how it is to be done. The dynamics of applying each form of engagement in the right proportion is what the leader has to be thoughtful and skillful about.

Tackling a Mediocre Culture

A mediocre culture is one in which there is the predominance of an attitude of showing average commitment to excellence, ethics, innovation, and best practices. A mediocre culture doesn't appreciate openness, engagement, innovative thinking, and high standards as value-adding elements. For leaders to bring about a difference in the internal culture of a firm, they need to understand the role of leadership behaviors that are regarded as determinants of organizational performance (De Lacerda, 2015). They need to understand that their efforts will be majorly geared towards three significant areas of behaviors and attitudes, i.e.

A. **Change-Oriented Behaviors:** Leaders who want to lead behavioral change in their organizations understand that it must start with them and that their leadership is a central factor in facilitating and engendering that change. The first thing they need to do is to effectively communicate a vision, carry their subordinates and TEAM members along in the transformation process, and encourage innovative thinking and openness. Communicating a compelling vision that inspires the TEAM and propels TEAM members to go the extra mile on the job is strategic to eliciting behavioral change. Through the shared vision, mission statement, goals, agenda, and common purpose of the group, TEAM members are also able to go through a process of identification, and this makes the desirable future state more graphic, while they better envision their roles in pursuit of the cause.

B. **Relational-Oriented Behaviors:** This is where the interpersonal abilities and people skills of the leader are tested. Leaders need to be able to get their followers and subordinates to commit to goals in a meaningful and personal way, which is why successful leaders employ such methods as empowering other members of the TEAM through delegation of authority and distribution of project tasks. These leaders are charismatic and energetic, which creates an atmosphere for their subordinates to identify with the leader's energy and take their cue from the leader's example. By getting people involved in a collective effort, engaging them in participatory strategic decisions, and infusing a motivating and energetic atmosphere through the compelling energy of the leader, their drive towards the collective task will be heightened. They will also become caught up with a healthy sense of importance, see a higher purpose, and feel an uplifting aspiration towards the invigorating achievements set before them.

When leaders empower their TEAMs like this and give them the tools they need to perform, the vision and sense of belonging created becomes a lively push for TEAM members, and this leads to a shift in the culture of the organization. It will also create cooperation and synergy and will deepen the level of interaction between members of the TEAM or organization. Trust, accountability, and capacity-building are the results of such an atmosphere, and the leaders would have succeeded in creating potential leaders across the rank and file.

C. **Task-Oriented Behaviors:** Task-oriented behaviors have to do with the standards of performance and delivery that leaders expect of their subordinates, employees, or other TEAM members. There is a need to clearly define what the standards are so that they can be part of the commitment and drive of followers as they undertake any set of tasks or projects. This influences the perception and behavior of employees towards the organization as a whole and also in relation to the performance of their responsibilities and assignments in connection with the organization. Where there are no clearly defined standards or where the standards are poorly set, it isn't difficult to anticipate that the potentials of the organization will remain unchallenged, and in many areas, untapped. Employees will then settle for average and just enough results to get by. This is how mediocrity sets in and becomes the operational ceiling.

It is therefore important that leaders set and communicate clear standards; see to it that their followers understand and are in concord with the standards; ensure that performance is appraised (for affirmation or correction, and for reward or punishment), and new goals are set or former goals reset in the unending cycle of corporate activities. While change and relational behaviors are more akin to charismatic and transformational leadership abilities, fostering the right task orientation is essentially transactional. While the leader expects a certain measure of performance, subordinates expect that when they do well, they are recognized or rewarded, and when they fall below expectation, they are corrected or punished. In this way, leaders serve as reinforcement for the right task-oriented behaviors in their followers, while the followers, through their performance or non-performance, are reinforcement for the leader's drive to promote and entrench these behaviors.

Change-Oriented Behaviors	Relational-Oriented Behaviors	Task-Oriented Behaviors
Communicate a compelling vision	Empower team members through delegation	Set and communicate clear standards of performance
Value statements help team members identify with vision	Leader's energy help others commit in a personal way	Reward and punishment serve as reinforcement

Fig 10.2 Major Behaviors Promoted by Leaders for Organizational Excellence

Kicking out mediocrity and creating a culture of excellence requires that leaders develop the capabilities of their staff or TEAM members to identify the core problem they are dealing with and to also point out the relevant skills and competencies required to meet the demands. For this to happen, the organization must have the following:

- Well-defined purpose and objectives
- The right structure
- Effective and efficient work tools
- A reward system

- Healthy relationships between co-workers and between subordinates and their leaders
- A robust leadership
- Good TEAMwork

The portrait of an organization that wants a culture of excellence and not mediocrity will look something like this:

1. Well-spelled-out purpose and value statements (i.e., vision, mission, and core values) that are adequately communicated to members of staff and the TEAM so that everyone has a good grasp of what the organization is about and are united in purpose.
2. Well highlighted areas of competitive advantage and business/corporate strategy.
3. Synergy and collaboration. Employees, units, and leaders of the organization work together towards the achievement of the long-term and short-term goals and objectives of the organization. They collaborate on different projects and in the performance of their daily functions.
4. High standards, competitive targets, and an emphasis on high performance. The company must set high ethical and work standards, competitive targets and emphasize high performance to its staff.
5. Encouragement of creativity, innovation, and entrepreneurial drive in order to ensure proactivity and responsiveness to market opportunities, realities, and changes.
6. Partnership and networking with people and organizations that have other areas of comparative advantage, technical expertise, and experience.
7. Venturing into new areas of opportunities, creating new products and services, modifying existing products and services, and enhancing delivery and value chains.

Three major steps and stages summarize the path an organization can take out of a mediocre culture into one of excellence.

The first stage is creating a paradigm of excellence in the organization. This is the most crucial stage in nurturing a culture of excellence and putting mediocrity at bay. Leaders must ensure that the consciousness of their people reflects excellence, a reach for the highest standards, and a drive for the finest pursuits. Where the people think small and have a mindset that accepts mediocre results, they will bring the organization down to the level of their thinking. It is better to raise the thinking and standard and let the organization catch up with it. This way, people are under positive pressure to give their best and to be creative and innovative.

The next stage is hatching the right strategies for excellence. Specific goals, plans, and regulations should be put in place to ensure that there are specific targets by which the organization can measure its performance. There should be laid-out plans to meet specific targets; and rules and regulations to uphold the vision, mission, core values, and objectives of the organization. Without well-thought-out strategies and regulations that help the organization to meet specific targets and its overall objectives, excellence will only be a pipe dream.

Finally, it is important that the organization has the right set of leaders who can drive the TEAM to achieve its goals. It all rises and falls on leadership, and as a result, if the organization doesn't have the right set of leaders who can lead from the front, motivate the TEAM, and who have the right skills and competencies to help the TEAM achieve its goals, then excellence will become elusive, and the company's goals and objectives will suffer from a lack of capable hands.

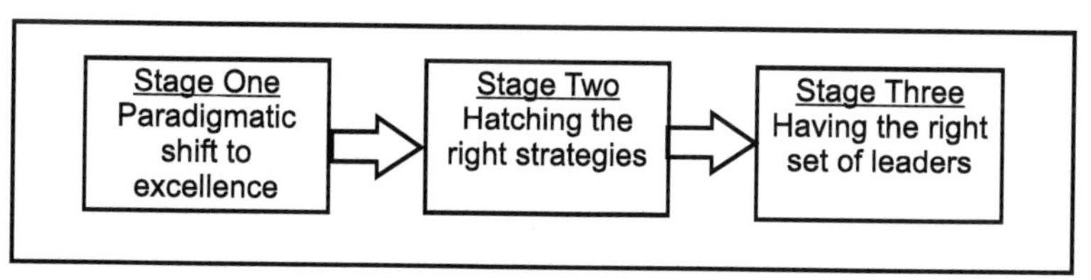

Fig 10.3 Stages for Tackling Mediocrity and Instilling Excellence

Avoiding Second-Rate Leadership

For organizations to have the best leadership, the first point they need to note is that they must have a clear picture of what qualities they want in a leader and what their expectations are in relation to the specific needs of the organization at that particular time and for the near future. Identifying the exact characteristics and itemizing the specific needs of the firm is the groundwork required to be able to profile the competencies, unique attributes, and skills that the job opening being recruited for requires. It is also important that founders and major stakeholders of organizations set a clear map for the organization that captures its current projects, long and short-term goals, organizational style and structures, values, and vision. This provides an immediate template for the incoming leader to work with before other strategies are developed.

When recruiting, it is important that organizations include in the job advert an adequate description of the job position; the responsibilities, demands, and activities that come with it; and what is expected of the incoming leader. Organizations should also stipulate the essential qualities, attributes, and competencies they expect to see in the leader. Furthermore, it is important to describe in the job advert the nature of the environment, organizational culture, industry-related expectations, and management philosophy in place in order to prepare the mind of the incoming leader and to portray a clear picture of the context in which the leader will operate. What taking these measures will do is to help potential recruits for the positions to assess whether they have what it takes to fit into the role and if they can deliver, knowing the rigors and expectations that come with the job. Mediocre leaders or those with inadequate skills will thus have an opportunity to evaluate the enormity of responsibilities, technicalities, and leadership skills required of them within the specified environment, and this could help them make an early decision to pass on the opportunity if they don't feel up to the task.

Measuring the track record of potential candidates is also a very crucial step at this stage. It is important that people are evaluated based on what they have done and not what they say they can do.

However, beyond the highlights of achievements on the résumés and CVs of potential candidates, organizations must also find ingenious ways during the recruitment and interview process to prove the abilities, skills, experience, and potentials of those they are reviewing for positions in their establishment. Today's business environments are tough, and it is important that organizations have a suitable role competency model that contains a clear description of the knowledge, skills, personal characteristics, and capabilities required for candidates to stand up to the challenges in the environment they are to work in (Mattone & Xavier 2013; Tredrea, 2018). Below are some of the competencies that organizations should look for in choosing excellent leaders:

1. **Critical thinking:** Leaders need to be able to consider diverse viewpoints, collect information from credible sources, and evaluate customer and stakeholder feedback before making a decision. Critical thinking requires that leaders recognize their own biases and not allow them to affect their thoroughness in evaluating the information available to them.

2. **Analytical in Decision-making:** Leaders should be able to give a good analysis of the options available to them and single out the most important factors that should lead to the final decision. Their ability to analyze will be handy in convincing stakeholders, enlightening the manage-ment TEAM, and propelling other members towards action.

3. **Ability to strategize:** Excellent leaders have a good grasp of their business, the market, their industry, and the organization's leverage and weaknesses. Based on these, they are able to develop strategies to help the business retain market relevance, stay competitive, achieve short and long-term goals, and effectively manage the internal affairs of the firm.

4. **Emotional intelligence:** Effective leaders understand the nuances of managing their emotions, interpreting those of others, and handling knotty situations involving members of the TEAM.

5. **Excellent communication abilities:** Communication is at the nerve of effective leadership. It is impossible to get leadership right if leaders are defective in their communication. Communicating clearly, listening attentively, and ensuring effective channels for feedback are vital to every leader's success.

6. **Passionate go-getter:** Great leaders are passionate about what they do, and they are focused on achieving set goals. They leave no stone unturned in pursuing their set objectives and do not get distracted. Their result-oriented approach to leadership keeps the TEAM energetic, focused, and innovative.

7. **Team player and developer:** Excellent leaders are great TEAM players! They work in groups, believe in TEAMwork, and know-how to identify themselves as part of a TEAM and not as isolated individuals. How well a leader can function with a TEAM will determine how far he can take the organization. As TEAM players, great leaders know the value of carrying the TEAM along, empowering people with authority and the tools they need, and ensuring that they give some level of independence to their staff instead of micromanaging them. Strong leaders are also good at building and developing TEAMs because of their ability to spot talent, get people to work together, and set the agenda to guide the TEAM.

8. **Talent management and coaching:** Strong leaders are able to effectively manage the talent under their care by providing a conducive environment and the right incentives for them to work. They ensure that the creative abilities of those who serve under them are well tapped while they coach greenhorns to develop their innate potentials and skills. Leaders who cannot manage talent will make it difficult for the organization to benefit from innovative thinking, ideas, and important skills.

9. **Process Management:** To effectively manage their corporate or business operations, the ability of a leader to manage processes is important. Process management involves finding better ways of optimizing, improving,

automating, and modeling the various processes within the organization to maximize output and operational efficiency. It helps to ensure processes are well-aligned, blueprints implemented, and that the rate of success is effectively measured.

10. **Project Management:** Leaders must show they are able to coordinate operations, methodologies, human resources, information flow, and the material resources in their charge in order to achieve specific project objectives at given periods.

11. **Change Management:** The essential goal of change management is to deploy the right techniques that help manage people's responses to change within the organization. It is the process adopted to help prepare and assist TEAM members in making the desired change. Five steps to consider in managing change include: initiating change and the relevant discussions; doing an impact analysis; approving the best measures after the impact analysis; implementing the change; and reviewing the process and its impact. Where necessary, make adaptations, which by the way are in themselves relevant changes, only that they are minor in nature.

12. **Information Management:** This involves effectively creating, sharing, using, and managing the knowledge and information among members of an organization. The process involves discovering and collecting data, organizing and evaluating data for organizational assimilation, applying the knowledge gained, disseminating the knowledge, and storing the information.

13. **Resource management:** This has to do with the effective and efficient use and allocation of resources to meet the needs and demands for productivity. Successful leaders show accountability, know how to prioritize, and ensure that resources are allocated in the most cost-effective manner.

14. **Results and milestones evaluation:** It is important to evaluate how often the leader shows a propensity to

assess the quality of results achieved and to monitor the milestone progressions? Leaders must have at the back of their minds the time frame, quality of results desired, and the big picture within which they are navigating their pursuits.

15. **Priority for learning:** Leaders who are not passionate about learning, willing to unlearn, and humble enough to relearn can't function in the 21st Century with its fast-paced changes, knowledge-intensive industries, and the quick obsolescence of knowledge that characterize it. Leaders must keep learning to remain on the cutting-edge of developments in their markets, industries, and socio-economic environment.

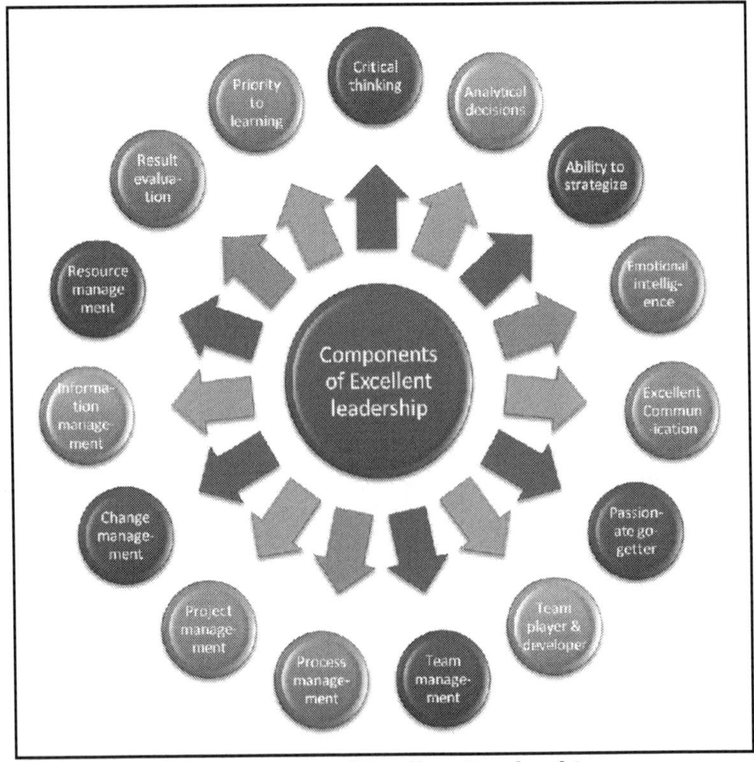

Fig 10.4 Vital Components of Excellent Leadership

It is important to reiterate that leaders must be people of integrity and must be accountable. Insisting on integrity and accountability are important components to curb incidences of abuse by leaders. Where leaders do not have systems in place to check them, ensure they are accountable, and make them live up to sound ethical principles, such leaders are prone to abuse their powers and privileges. The highlighted qualities above are fundamental to avoiding second-rate leadership, and looking out for them will help bring on board high performing and excellent leaders.

CONCLUSION

In conclusion, the propositions and analyses that have been extensively treated in the course of this book point to cogent inferences and analyses about the nature of mediocre leadership and its impact on businesses, corporate bodies, and groups. One of such inferences is that mediocre leadership and mediocre cultures are mutually reinforcing agents in the life cycle of organizations. A mediocre leader, by default, will superintend over an organization in such a manner that it literally takes on his image; interestingly, the paradox earlier noted in this book is that most mediocre leaders are products of their organizations and have actually emerged through the system. In other words, they are only a reflection of the culture, values, and nature of the organizations that produced them. Unfortunately, a high-performance culture must begin at the top of an organization and trickle down to its other layers, but since most leaders in the corporate world are promoted in turns or for other subjective reasons outside of their proven leadership capabilities, mediocre leadership has become rife. Leaders who rise to positions that are above their skills, experience, and capabilities are less likely to provide inspiring leadership—especially at strategic and delicate times.

Mediocre leaders also lack the focal pivot of leadership, which is the ability to source, effectively manage, and efficiently propel human and material resources towards excellence and the achievement of set goals, objectives, and vision. As a result of their ineptitude, they absorb themselves more in their comfort zone, promote conservatism, are closed-minded, and are ineffective in communicating the vision in a way that propels the TEAM. Mediocre leaders may also develop self-centered traits, could often pass the buck, or condescend to playing the politics of inversion in which the talented are marginalized (or are prevented from being recruited into the organization), while the less able are clandestinely favored. Unfortunately for these leaders, the 21st-century has proven to be one in which knowledge obsolescence gaps are constantly being created due to the ever-changing innovation landscape in various industries and markets. It is therefore important that leaders being prospected for specific job roles are evaluated based on the skills needed in the roles they are being interviewed for. This is vital to sustaining excellence and curtailing the chances of recycling mediocre leaders.

In the course of this book, light has been shed on the value of theoretical and practical knowledge to the success of leadership. A leader's deficiency in required areas of theoretical and practical knowledge makes the leader inadequate, and this inadequacy could constitute a costly liability to the fortunes of the firm. For instance, the explicit theoretical knowledge gained from R&D undertakings, and the implicit knowledge created within an organization due to the high quality of human capital available, are some of the indispensable components of the competitive advantage that the organization needs to deploy against competitors and to survive in a tough environment. Knowledge is vital to success, and when it is successfully applied to achieve specific ends, it is due to the ability of the leader to turn theoretical knowledge into practical usage—this in itself is also a critical factor in leadership. However, the earlier discourse on the Peter Principle further reveals the importance of continuous training for leaders, especially in the 21st Century, characterized by a high degree of knowledge obsolescence. The Peter Principle posits that people in a hierarchical system tend to get promoted until they reach their level of incompetence. This implies that a posture of continuous learning in line with the four stages of the conscious competence model discussed in chapter two is crucial for leaders who want to stay current and relevant. Conscious competence positively impacts the cognitive abilities of leaders and could also be an effective tool in shaping their metacognition.

Cognitive and metacognitive skills are essential to fostering effective communication and a good understanding of the decision-making process. The cognitive ability of the leader helps during communication to elicit the right cognitive, interactive, and expressive response from TEAM members, which in turn leads to identifying the right decision and course of action. Metacognition, on the other hand, helps the leader gain effective control of his cognitive assessments in relation to concrete objectives by drawing on past experiences of similar tasks or situations to generate a decision framework and appropriately adapt the same to resolving the new task at hand. This enhances the decision-making model of leaders and helps them to stand on a pedestal that is higher than mediocre or average. Apart from these competence-based deficiencies that mediocre leaders grapple with, there are also ethical and personality defects that characterize their administration and which contribute to the deficits in their leadership. Mediocre leaders who fight to secure their positions in the organization tend to pander to unfounded, erroneous, and spurious arguments in order to morally disengage. Moral disengagement, therefore, becomes a ploy that they use to induce relief from the internal self-distress and burden of their immoral conduct. It is these disengagement practices that diminish their self-restraint until inhumane practices become thoughtlessly normalized.

When leaders cross the ethical line, they disregard moral principles, relegate best practices to the background, and flout legal provisions and organizational rules. They also become rigid, resistant to change, and unwelcoming to new ideas—except for those ideas that promote their selfish agenda. These Mediocre leaders tend to show inconsistency in their managerial practices, can be people-pleasers, play favoritism, and due to their low metacognition, are more erratic in making strategic decisions when operating in highly competitive environments. They are also often afraid to lose their positions to more competent hands, and therefore become pathological controllers, chronic micro-managers, and unsympathetic leaders. This deficit in people skills makes it impracticable for such leaders to inspire their employees during difficult times or to connect with them through effective communication. The atmosphere created by the unethical conduct of mediocre leadership strains the culture of an organization, diminishes collectivism, and adversely affects other organizational citizenship behaviors (OCB). This is a reflection of individualistic, narrow-minded, and self-centered leadership. And just as it has been noted in chapter eight, self-centered leaders thrive on the tripod of personalism, individualism, and pseudo-institutionalism.

Finally, it is important to mention that the antidote to mediocre leadership is to instill a culture of excellence and to avoid appointing second-rate leaders to positions of leadership. Instilling a culture of excellence will require taking the organization through change-oriented behaviors, relational-oriented behaviors, and task-oriented behaviors. These behavioral considerations should be geared towards engendering a paradigmatic and actionable framework within which employees can effectively pursue the well-laid-out vision, mission, goals, and objectives of the business or organization. However, after this groundwork, it is important that only resourceful leaders with critical and analytical minds, emotional intelligence, excellent communication skills, and other vital competencies such as proven abilities in resource, process, and TEAM management, etc., are allowed to mount the saddle of leadership. Dogmatic individuals who operate from narrow inclinations will find it difficult to incorporate such progressive shifts despite the logical and credible reasons for them to do so. Such persons are slow to recognize bad outcomes, are culturally discordant, and primordially insular. They will constitute a slur to the organization's progress and will reinvent the cycle of mediocrity. The organization should ventilate its system by allowing such people an opportunity to leave and allowing others with fresh insights, energy, and ideas to come on board.

REFERENCES

Aboyassin, Naser A., and Abood, Najim (2013). "The effect of ineffective leadership on individual and organizational performance in Jordanian institutions." Competitiveness Review: An International Business Journal Vol. 23 No. 1, pp. 68-84 © Emerald Group Publishing Limited 1059-5422. DOI 10.1108/10595421311296632

Adams, Linda. "Learning a new skill is easier said than done." gordontraining.com. Gordon Training International. Retrieved 21 May 2011.

Appelbaum, Steven H., and Roy-Girard, David (2007). "Toxins in the workplace: affect on organizations and employees." Corporate Governance, Vol. 7 NO. 1 pp. 17-28. © Emerald Group Publishing Limited. ISSN 1472-0701. DOI 10.1108/14720700710727087.

Ashworth, K. (2001). "Caught between the dog and the fireplug, or how to survive in public service." Washington, DC: Georgetown University Press.

Avey, J., Wernsing, T., & Palanski, M. (2012). "Exploring the process of ethical leadership: The mediating role of employee voice and psychological ownership." Journal of BusinessEthics, 107, 21-34.

Bandura, A. (1999). Moral disengagement in the perpetuation of inhumanities. Personality and Social Psychology Review, 3, 193-209.

Berman, E. M., West J.P. (2003). "What is managerial mediocrity? Definition, Prevalence, and Negative Impact (Part 1)." Public Performance & Management Review, Vol. 27 No. 2, December 2003, pp. 9–29.© 2004 M.E. Sharpe, Inc. All rights reserved.

Bradberry, Travis, and Greaves, Jean (2005). "Heartless Bosses." Harvard Business Review. Available at https://hbr.org/2005/12/heartless-bosses

Brandon, W. Jones (2011). "Leadership Consistency." Copyright © · Brandon W. Jones · Leadership Done Right. Published online (June 1, 2011) at https://leadershipdoneright.com/leadership-consistency/

Brooke Meredith (2019). "Why Most Managers are Mediocre at Best, and How We Might Shift This for the Better." Published by Medium, available at https://medium.com/@brookemeredith/why-most-managers-are-mediocre-at-best-and-how-we-might-shift-this-for-the-better-c610f2312376.

Brown, M. E., Mitchell, M. S., 2010. Ethical and unethical leadership: Exploring new avenues for future research. Business Ethics Quarterly, Vol. 20, pp. 583–616.

Bonita Richter (2018). "Change Management: Barriers to Why Leaders Resist Change." Published online by Profit Strategies (March 16, 2018).

Brown, T., Sautter, J., Littvay, L., Sautter, A., & Bearnes, B. (2010). Ethics and personality: Empathy and narcissism as moderators of ethical decision making in business students. Journal of Education for Business, 85(4), 203–208.

Charles A. O'Reilly III, Michael L. Tushman (2016). "Lead and Disrupt: How to Solve the Innovator's Dilemma." Stanford Business Books, 1st Edition.

Clancy, Annette (2018). "How to stop being a people-pleaser." Manage and Lead Journal, Vol. 50, p.67.

David Dunning, Kerri Johnson, Joyce Ehrlinger, and Justin Kruger (2003). "Why People Fail to Recognize Their Own

Incompetence." Current Directions in Psychological Science, Vol.12 (3), American Psychology Society.

Dávila, M.C., & Finkelstein, M.A. (2010). Predicting organizational citizenship behavior from the functional analysis and role identity perspectives: Further evidence in Spanish employees. Spanish Journalof Psychology, 13(1), 277-283.

Devay, M. (2010). Empathy: A multidisciplinary approach. Dissertation, Georgetown University, District of Columbia, United States. Retrieved November 17, 2010, from Dissertations & Theses: Full Text (Publication No. AAT 1475426).

De Lacerda, Teresa Correia (2015). "Understanding leadership effectiveness in organizational settings: An integrative approach." ISEG School of Management and Economics, University de Lisboa. DOI: 10.13140/RG.2.1.2870.1289

De León, M. C. D., & Finkelstein, M. A. (2011). "Individualism/ collectivism and organizational citizenship behavior." Psicothema Vol. 23, No. 3, pp. 401-406

DeRue Scott D. and Ned Wellman (2009). "Developing Leaders via Experience: The Role of Developmental Challenge, Learning Orientation, and Feedback Availability." Journal of Applied Psychology Vol. 94, No. 4, 859–875 0021-9010/09/$12.00 DOI: 10.1037/a0015317. © 2009 American Psychological Association.

Diana Rus, Daan van Knippenberg, Barbara Wisse (2010). Leader power and self-serving leader behavior: The role of effective leadership beliefs and performance information. Journal of Experimental Social Psychology, Elsevier, 46 (6), pp.922. 10.1016/j.jesp.2010.06.007. hal-00864368.

Dina Gerdeman (2016). "How Rigid Leaders Kill their Companies."

HBS Working Knowledge, Leadership Strategy. Business research for business leaders. Published online by Forbes, on September 26, 2016.

Edwards, Lee (2017)."Consistency and Inconsistency in Organizations: A DialecticalPerspective." Management Communication Quarterly, Vol. 31 (3). pp. 486-491. ISSN0893-3189. Available at https://doi.org/10.1177/0893318917700295.

E. M. Berman, J.P. West "WHAT IS MANAGERIAL MEDIOCRITY? Definition, Prevalence, and Negative Impact (Part 1)." Public Performance & Management Review, Vol. 27 No. 2, December 2003, pp. 9–29. © 2004 M.E. Sharpe, Inc. All rights reserved.

Einarsen, S., Aasland. M. S., Skogstad, A., (2007). Destructive leadership behavior: A definition and conceptual model. The Leadership Quarterly Vol. 18,pp. 207–216.

Eisenberg, S. A., Brodbeck, F. (2014). "Ethical and unethical leadership: A cross-cultural and cross-sectoral analysis." Journal of Business Ethics Vol. 122,pp. 343–359.

Edwin Bosso (2020). "5 Reasons Company Leaders Resist Needed Change – Even During This Crisis." Published online by Global Trade Mag. (July 16, 2020). www.globaltrademag.com%2F5-reasons-company-leaders-resist-needed-change-even-during-this-crisis%2F

Flavell JH. (, 1976). "Metacognitive aspects of problemsolving." In The Nature of Intelligence, Resnick LR(Ed). Erlbaum: Hillsdale, NJ; pp. 231–235.

FMI (2010). "The Isolated Executive: from larger than life to real, engaging and inspiring." © 2010 FMI Corporation. Available at https://www.fminet.com/wp-content/uploads/2017/04/The-Isolated-Executive.pdf.

Green, Eva G. T., Deschamps Jean-Claude, and Páez Dario (2005). "Variation of Individualism andCollectivism within and between 20 Countries: A Typological Analysis." Journal of Cross-Cultural Psychology, Vol. 36 No. 3, pp. 321-339.© Sage Publications.DOI: 10.1177/0022022104273654.

Gustavo Guzman (2009). "What Is Practical Knowledge?" Journal of Knowledge ManagementVol. 13 No. 4, 2009, Pp. 86-98, Emerald Group Publishing Limited, Issn 1367-367-3270 DOI 10.1108/13673270910971851

Hammad, W. and Norris, N. (2009), "Centralized control: a barrier to shared decision-making in Egyptian secondary school," International Studies in Educational Administration, Vol. 37 No. 2, pp. 60-73.

Hannah, S.T., Lester, P.B., and Vogelgesang, G.R. (2005). "Moral Leadership: Explicating the Moral Component of Authentic Leadership." Authentic Leadership Theory and Practice: Origins, Effects, and Development Monographs in Leadership and Management, Volume 3, 43–81. Copyright2005 by Elsevier Ltd.

Hansen, Alice (2012). "Trainees and teachers as reflective learners." In Hansen, Alice; et al. (eds.). Reflective learning and teaching in primary schools. London; Thousand Oaks, CA: Learning Matters; Sage Publications, Vol. 34 pp. 32–48.

Hawass, Hisham H. (2019). "The riddle of self-centered leadership in Arab organizations: a measurement scale." Management Research Review Vol. 42 No. 4, pp. 430-459 © Emerald Publishing Limited, 2040-8269.DOI 10.1108/MRR-04-2018-0168.

Haynie M., Shepherd D.A. (2009). "A measure of adaptivecognition for entrepreneurship research." EntrepreneurshipTheory and Practice Vol. 33(3), pp. 695–714.

Heidrich, Balázs and Réthi, Gábor (2012). "Services and Service Management." In Delener, N. (Ed). "Service Science Research, Strategy and Innovation: Dynamic Knowledge Management Methods." Business Science Reference, Copyright © 2012, IGI Global. DOI: 10.4018/978-1-4666-0077-5.ch001.

Hersey, P.H., Blanchard, K.H., Johnson, D.E (2015). Management of Organizational Behavior – Leading Human Resources, 10th ed. Pearson Education: Upper Saddle River.

Holt, Svetlana, and Marques, Joan (2012). "Empathy in Leadership: Appropriate or Misplaced? An Empirical Study on a Topic that is asking for Attention." Journal of Business EthicsVol. 105, pp. 95–105. DOI 10.1007/s10551-011-0951-5.

Hugh Blane (2017). "Why Leaders Resist Change." Published online by CU Management (July 03, 2017). © Credit Union Executives Society (CUES). Available at https://www.cumanagement.com/connect/skybox/2017/07/03/why-leaders-resist-change.

Inzlicht, Michael, and Obhi, Sukhvinder (2014). "Powerful and Coldhearted." The New York Times (Sunday Review). http://www.nytimes.com/2014/07/27/opinion/sunday/powerful-and-coldhearted.html?_r=0.

Isabel, A. (2011). The impact of market orientation dimensions on client cooperation in the development of new service innovations. European Journal of Marketing. p. 43 – 67.

Ibbotson, Steven (2018). "The Insular organization." Available at https://stevenibbotson.wordpress.com/2018/12/11/the-insular-organization/

Izenberg, D. (2007). Does therapy belong in class? Maclean's, 119 (52–53), pp.34–35.

John Schwenkler (2015). "Understanding 'Practical Knowledge. " Philosophers' Imprint, Vol. 15, No. 15, pp.1-32.

Jonathan Grudin (2016). "The Rise of Incompetence." Microsoft research, ACM Interactions, Vol. 23, pp. 6-7. Available at https://www.microsoft.com/en-us/research/wp-content/uploads/2017/01/the-rise-of-incompetence.pdf

Joseph C. Hermanowicz (2013). "The culture of mediocrity." Minerva, 2013, Vol. 51, pp.363-387

Karelaia N, Hogarth R.M. (2008). "Determinants of linear judgment: a meta-analysis of lens model studies." Psychological Bulletin 134(3),pp. 404–426.

Kellerman, Barbara (2014). "Insular Leadership – the Case of Barack Obama." © Barbara Kellerman. Available at https://barbarakellerman.com/insular-leadership-the-case-of-barack-obama/

Khadra, B. (1990), "The prophetic-caliphal model of leadership: an empirical study," International Studies of Management and Organization, Vol. 20, No. 3, pp. 37-51.

Knight, Rebecca (2017). "How Managers Can Avoid Playing Favorites." © Harvard Business Review (March 15, 2017). Available at https://hbr.org/2017/03/how-managers-can-avoid-playing-favorites.

Lašáková, A., Remišová, A. (2015)."Unethical Leadership: Current Theoretical Trends and Conceptualization." Procedia Economics and Finance,Vol. 34, pp. 319 – 328.

Laurie Maddalena (2019). "Five signs you have a mediocre culture." Published by CU Insight, available at https://www.cuinsight.com/five-signs-you-have-a-mediocre-culture.html

Mahsud, R., Yukl, G., & Prussia (2010). Leader empathy, ethical leadership, and relations-oriented behaviors as antecedents of leader-member exchange quality. Journal of Managerial Psychology, 25(6), pp. 561–577.

Marcel Schwantes (2018). "Want to Avoid Being a Mediocre Manager? Start Displaying These 3 Rare Behaviors." Published by Inc. Available at https://www.inc.com/marcel-schwantes/the-quickest-way-to-great-leadership-wont-happen-without-improving-these-3-people-skills.html.

Mas-Machuca, M. (2014). "The Role of Leadership: The Challenge of Knowledge Management and Learning in Knowledge-Intensive Organizations." Journal of Educational Leadership and Management, Vol. 2(1), 97-116 doi: 10.4471/ijelm. 2014.10.

Matta. F. K., Scott. B. A., Colquitt. J. A., Koopman. J., and Passantino. L. G. (2016). "Is Consistently Unfair Better than Sporadically Fair? An Investigation of Justice Variability and Stress." Academy of Management Journal. Vol. 60, No. 2. pp. Available at https://doi.org.10.5465/amj.2014.0455.

Mattone, J., M., Xavier, L., X., Talent Leadership, 1601 Broadway, New York 10019.

Mayer, D. M., Aquino, K., Greenbaum, R. L., & Kuenzi, M. (2012). "Who displays ethical leadership and why does it matter? An examination of antecedents and consequences of ethical leadership." Academy of Management Journal, 55, 151-171.

Mayer, D. M., Kuenzi, M., Greenbaum, R., Bardes, M., & Salvador, R. (2009). "How low does ethical leadership flow? Test of a trickle-down model." Organizational Behavior and Human Decision Processes, 108, 1-13.

Mitchell, Robert J., Shepherd, Dean A., Sharfman, Mark P., (2011). "Erratic Strategic Decisions: When and Why Managers are Inconsistent in Strategic Decision Making." Strategic

Management Journal. Vol. 32, pp. 683–704. DOI: 10.1002/smj.905.

Michael C Bush, "The Leadership Quality that Separates Mediocre Bosses from Great Ones." Speakers Office. https://www.speakersoffice.com/the-leadership-quality-that-separates-mediocre-bosses-from-great-ones/

Moore, C., Mayer, D.M., Chiang, F.T., Crossley, C.D., Karlesky, M.J., Birtch, T.T.A. (2018). "Leaders Matter Morally: The Role of Ethical Leadership in Shaping Employee Moral Cognition and Misconduct." Journal of Applied Psychology (June 2018), pp.1-70, DOI:10.1037/apl0000341

Montgomery, Peter S. (1972). "Belief-Disbelief Systems and Security-Insecurity." https://ttu-ir.tdl.org/bitstream/handle/2346/20349/31295015065435.pdf?sequence=1

Moorman, R.H., & Blakely, G.L. (1995). Individualism-collectivism, as an individual difference predictor of organizational citizenship behavior. Journal of Organizational Behavior, 16, 127-142.

Natalie Mizik and Robert Jacobson (2007). "The Cost of Myopic Management." Published online by Harvard Business Review athttps://hbr.org/2007/07/the-cost-of-myopic-management-2.

Ng, T. W. H., & Feldman, D. C. (2015). Ethical leadership: Meta-analytic evidence of criterion-related and incremental validity. Journal of Applied Psychology, 100, 948–965.

Nicol, A.A.M. (2009), "Social dominance orientation, right-wing authoritarianism, and their relation with leadership styles." Personality and Individual Differences, Vol. 47 No. 6, pp. 657-661.

Ohlott, P. J. (2004). "Job assignments." In C. McCauley & E. V. Velsor

(Eds.), The Center for Creative Leadership handbook of leadership development (2nd ed., pp. 151–182). San Francisco: Jossey-Bass.

Olukunle A. Iyanda (2020). "Dismantling Organizational Rigidity: The effect of Strategy, Structure and Culture Change." Broot Consulting: Strategy | Innovation | Research. Available at https://brootc.com//our-blog/innovation/design-thinking/dismantling-organisational-rigidity-idea-generation/

Oyserman, D., Coon, H.M., & Kemmelmeier, M. (2002). Rethinking individualism and collectivism: Evaluation of theoretical assumptions and meta-analyses. Psychological Bulletin, 128(1), 3-72.

Petra Koudelková, (2015). "The Significance of Theoretical Knowledge for Business Innovation." Mediterranean Journal of Social Sciences, MCSER Publishing, Rome-Italy. DOI: 10.5901/mjss.2015.v6n6p325.

Pless, N. M., Maak, T. (2011). "Responsible leadership: Pathways to the future." Journal of Business Ethics Vol. 98, pp. 3–13.

Philip Liebman (2016). "7 Symptoms of a Mediocre Organization, And How Leadership Can Restore Health." Available at https://www.linkedin.com/pulse/7-symptoms-mediocre-organization-how-leadership-can-liebman-mlas/

Poorkavoos, Meysam (2016). "Compassionate Leadership: What is it, and why do Organizations need more of it? © Roffey Park Institute." Available at https://www.roffeypark.ac.uk/wp-content/uploads/2020/07/Compassionate-Leadership-Booklet.pdf

Rick Whiting (2010). "Who Is Leo ApothekerAnd What Is His Channel Track Record?" CRN: News, Analysis, and Perspective for Solution Providers and Technology Integrators. © 2020 The Channel Company.

Robert E. Wenig (2004). "Leadership Knowledge and Skill: An Enabler for Success as a Technology Education Teacher-Leader." The Journal of Technology Studies, Vol. 30 (1/2), pp. 59-64.

Rokeach, M (1954). "The nature and meaning of dogmatism." Psychology Review, Vol.61, pp. 194-204.

Rokeach, M (1960). "The open and closed mind." New York: Basic Books, Inc.

Rokeach, M., McGovney, W. C., & Denny, M. R. (1955). "A distinction between dogmatic and rigid thinking." Journal of Abnormal and Social Psychology, Vol. 51, pp. 87-93.

Rokeach, M., McGovney, W. C., & Denny, M. R. (1960). "Dogmatic thinking versus rigid thinking: An experimental distinction." In M. Rokeach, The open and closed mind. New York: Basic Books, Inc.

Rosiński, Jerzy (2017). "The Negative Organizational Consequences of Average Leadership Skills. Case Studies Based on Ken Blanchard's Paradigm." International Journal of Contemporary Management Vol. 16 No. 4, pp. 165–184. doi:10.4467/24498939IJCM.17.043.8266

Saunders, Elizabeth .G. (2012). "Stop Being a People-Pleaser." © Harvard Business Review (October 30, 2012). Available at https://hbr.org/2012/10/stop-being-a-people-pleaser.

Schein, Edgar. H. (2015). "Leadership: What Is Old and What Is NEW?" In: Trilogue Salzburg (Ed)In Search of Leadership –A Critical Requirement for Governance, Social Cohesion, and Competitiveness (pp. 14-21). Published by Bertelsmann Stiftung. Available at: https://www.bertelsmannstiftung.

de/fileadmin/files/Projekte/84_Salzburger_Trilog/Analyse_Salzburger_Trilog_Leadership_What_Is_Old_and_What_Is_New_20150806.pdf; letzterZugriff: 08.10.2015).

Schein, Edgar. H. (2015). "Leadership: What Is Old and What Is NEW?" In: Trilogue Salzburg (Ed) In Search of Leadership –A Critical Requirement for Governance, Social Cohesion, and Competitiveness (pp. 14-21). Published by Bertelsmann Stiftung. Available at: https://www.bertelsmann stiftung.de/fileadmin/files/Pr ojekte/84_Salzburger_Trilog/Analyse_Salzburger_Trilog_Leadership_What_Is_Old_and_What_Is_New_20150806.pdf; letzterZugriff: 08.10.2015).

Schraw, G., Dennison R.S. (1994). "Assessing metacognitive awareness." Contemporary Educational Psychology 19(4): pp. 460–475.

Schwartz, M.S. (2005)."Universal Moral Values for Corporate Codes of Ethics." Journal of Business Ethics Vol. 59, No. 1/2 pp. 27-44. Published by Springer.

Sherrie Campbell (2014). "A Rigid Mind Blocks Success. Try These 5 Strategies for Fearless Leadership." Published online by Entrepreneur Media, Inc (November 21, 2014).

Stephanie, Mead (2020). "Broadening Your Horizons: Developing Open-Mindedness as a Leader." © 2020 Center for Management & Organization Effectiveness (CMOE). Published online at https://cmoe.com/blog/developing-open-mindedness-as-leader/

Steve Tobak (2012). "Why Leaders Resist Change." Published online in CBS News (Money Watch), April 16, 2012. Copyright © 2020 CBS Interactive Inc.

Suciu, Marta-Christina (2017). "The culture of excellence: Challenges and opportunities during changing times."

Proceedings of the 11th International Conference on Business Excellence (PICBE), pp. 322-331. ISSN 2558-9652. DOI: 10.1515/picbe-2017-0034.

Tomkins, L., and Simpson, P. (2015) Caring leadership: A Heideggerian perspective. Organization Studies. ISSN 0170-8406. Available at http://dx.doi.org/10.1177/ 017084061 5580008.

Tu, Y., & Lu, X. (2013). How ethical leadership influences employees' innovative work behavior: A perspective of intrinsic motivation. Journal of Business Ethics, 116, 441-455.

Tredrea, Andrea (2018). "How to Identify Potential Leaders Internally and Train them for Success." © University of Applied Sciences, Yrkeshögskolan, Novia. Available at https://core.ac.uk/download/pdf/161422623.pdf.

Vince Molinaro (2019). "Death by Mediocre Leadership: How Bad Leaders Are Sucking the Life Out of Your Company." Published by LHH. Available at https://www.lhh.com/ch/fr/organizations/article-listing/death-by-mediocre-leadership).

Whetten, D. A., & Cameron, K. S. (2016). "Developing Management Skills." 9th Edition, Essex, UK: Pearson Education Limited.

Wickham Skinner, and W. Earl Sasser (1977)."Versatile and Inconsistent." © Harvard Business Review (November 1977). Available at https://hbr.org/1977/11/versatile-and-inconsistent.

Weinstein, M., (July 2009). "Emotional evaluation." Training Magazine, pp. 20–23.

Zammit-Lucia, Joseph (2015). "Cultural Leadership: Towards a Cultural Leadership for the 21st Century; How leadership teams can succeed in the culture of our times." In Camunico Annual, Vol. 1, pp. 8-15. © Camunico, 2015. Available at http://camunico.com/wp-content/uploads/2015/10/Camunico-Annual-1.pdf

Made in the USA
Columbia, SC
22 July 2022